Activities for
Motivating and Teaching
Bright Children

Also by the Author:
Successful Techniques for Teaching Elementary Language Arts — Parker Publishing Co., Inc. — 1970

Activities for
Motivating and Teaching
Bright Children

by

Rosalind Minor Ashley

**Parker Publishing
Company, Inc.**

**West Nyack,
New York**

Library of Congress Cataloging in Publication Data

Ashley, Rosalind Minor.
   Activities for motivating and teaching bright
children.

   Includes bibliographical references.
   1. Gifted children—Education. 2. Student
activities. I. Title.
LC3993.2.A83   371.9'56   73-7776
ISBN 0-13-003624-2

Printed in the United States of America

Dedication

To my family, Chuck, Steve, and Rick Ashley,
and Fay and Jack Minor.

How This Book
Will Help You Develop
the Talents of Each Child

All children possess a gift or talent that we can value. In some cases, the aptitudes reflect a deep interest. In others, they are unusual abilities that can make these children contribute to the welfare of others — and to the quality of their own lives. This book will help you find and develop the special talents of all children. It will provide many activities in order to accomplish this end. The terms *bright* and *gifted* will be used interchangeably to describe these talents.

Activities are provided not only for the verbally bright, but for children who are talented in many other ways. These experiences will stimulate and give new direction to the many bored children who may be masking their brightness with destructive behavior. Most of these ideas will be useful for all pupils.

This book will describe the many ways that children can be bright. There are, of course, many other subject areas and many other kinds of talent. For each particular type of brightness mentioned here a special "club" will be suggested.

It is possible that some children will belong to two or three of these special groups at one time or another, possibly dropping out of one that was joined because of interest rather than special talent. One club can meet each day during an independent study time.

There are so many ways children can be bright that it is a certainty that each child can be legitimately brought into a special talent club of some kind. It will take time and effort to decide which children are definitely in a club and which ones can be encouraged to join if they wish. However, this is an important part of individualizing instruction. These special-interest clubs can provide the challenge and enrichment that only certain children need in some areas.

You may have the knowledge and talent to start and help with other clubs not mentioned in this book. For example, you may be able to work well with a special club for children with talent and interest in music.

There can be a few children who seem to have no special gifts or talents. They might not even show a strong interest in any subject. Rather than leave them out of a special group, help these pupils select the club that comes closest to their main interest, and let them get what they can from it. If you talk to them a lot, they'll let you know what they care about. It is possible that talent will develop later after exposure to certain types of activities. There are very few children who do not enjoy some type of music, dramatics, or handicraft, even if they show no inclination toward anything else.

There is nothing wrong with allowing a child who seems very interested to try out a club for a while. If he has no talent or real interest in the subject or activities, he will get bored and want to drop out on his own. He need not be excluded, except by encouraging him to join another group.

Exclusion is no problem. It *can* be a problem if a child has a talent and we do not realize it. This finding of hidden talent can take time, and we can miss some of it, but all you can do is follow every hint given you and try your best.

Make extensive use of achievement tests, but most judgments will have to be made on the basis of observation and trial and error. No harm will be done if a child who is mechanically inept accidentally gets into the club for the mechanically able. He may benefit the rest of his life from what he learns there about tools.

If you expect some students to stay in certain special-talent clubs and keep other membership extremely fluid based on interest, you will be able to meet the needs of the very gifted, and still provide interesting activities for the many slightly above-average children in different fields who have strong or changing special interests.

Individualized materials are needed for all talented pupils, but especially for the verbally bright. Most good educational programs are providing some of this enrichment. To meet the needs of the verbally gifted, we must provide much more. Because few teachers have the time to plan and write special materials, this book provides a sample programmed section written in the *scrambled* style. It can be easily adapted to any grade level or subject area to give needed stimulation. Simple charts and instructions show you how to scramble pages so that the brightest child cannot lose interest in the lesson or "beat the book" by peeking ahead. These programmed materials will amuse as well as enrich, because they contain a fun element that will maintain high interest. With a few modifications, the scrambled programmed approach will also be useful for children who are not verbally bright but who have special talents in certain fields.

Fun in school has now become respectable, and few teachers have to justify the planned use of games any longer. This book gives you two original games that may be used for motivating the study of maps and globes, and the study of ecology and health. The main elements of games are analyzed in a simple way for those who may wish to construct similar types of games for their own special-interest groups. These games can focus attention on a particular study, and will lead some pupils into research and deeper learning.

The ideas in this book are based on experiences in my own classroom, and on the activities going on in various other classrooms today. These methods have already been successful with numerous children. I have also used the latest studies on the gifted as the basis for creating new ideas, planned for the needs of our *many* bright children.

Rosalind Minor Ashley

ACKNOWLEDGMENTS

I am grateful for the help and suggestions given by Chuck, Steve, and Rick Ashley; Fay and Jack Minor; Dr. William J. Fritsche, Assistant Superintendent of Schools, District #39, Wilmette, Illinois; Joyce Arkin, Weber Elementary School, Parkway School District, Creve Coeur, Missouri; Peggy Pressley, Middlefork School, Sunset Ridge School District #29, Northfield, Illinois; Audrey Werner, Middlefork School, Sunset Ridge School District #29, Northfield, Illinois; Margaret Goldman, Middlefork School, Sunset Ridge School District #29, Northfield, Illinois; Kasia Stoloski, Grade 3, Middlefork School, Sunset Ridge School District #29; Ruth Ann Hodnett, Clarendon Hills, Illinois; Janet Yearout, Enhanced Learning Program for Gifted, Pinellas County Schools, Clearwater, Florida; Laura Joseph, Chicago, Illinois; Gail Carmichael, Grade 6, Glenview, Illinois; Robin Procunier, Grade 6, Glenview, Illinois; Alice Carmichael and John Carmichael, Glenview, Illinois; Donna Secrist, Librarian and Coordinator, Willard School, District #65, Evanston, Illinois; Mary Osborne, Principal, Middlefork School, Sunset Ridge School District #29, Northfield, Illinois; Helen Mitchell, Librarian, Middlefork School, Sunset Ridge School District #29, Northfield, Illinois; Martha Boos, Sunset Ridge School, Sunset Ridge School District #29, Northfield, Illinois; Maria Rauhauser, Instructional Materials Center, District #39, Wilmette, Illinois; Harriette Crummer, Director of Instructional Materials, Instructional Materials Center, District #39, Wilmette, Illinois; Dr. David A. Hagstrom, Principal, Willard School, District #65, Evanston, Illinois; Janice Conner, Maureen Ford, and Betty Ann Trainer, Willard School, District #65, Evanston, Illinois; and Martha Brannan, Moos School, Chicago, Illinois.

R.M.A.

Table of Contents

Who are they? How to recognize them. . . . Using
humor. . . . Composing limericks—a contest. . . . Planning puzzles. . . . Creating beauty in words—haiku. . . .
Using analogies. . . . Class previewers. . . . Preparing
living biographies—shadow voices. . . . How to use a card
catalogue to motivate wide reading. . . . Interest inventories. . . . More sample lessons. . . . Wanting to
write. . . . The Calm and Quiet Debating Society—a
club. . . . Checklist.

A simple plan of action. . . . Suggestions for writing
Behavioral Instructional Objectives that work for
you. . . . Sample Pre-Test and Post-Test. . . . How to use
the sample section for your own needs. . . . How to
scramble an intrinsic programmed booklet—a bubble
diagram. . . . Checklist.

Suggestions for identifying them.... "Community
Treasure Hunt".... "Mapdown" game.... "Blind
Man's Travels".... "Where Am I?".... Postcards from
imaginary travels. ... How to play "Grab-a-State"....
Adding interest to economics.... Using music....
Learning from buzz sessions.... World Pen Pals.... A
sample lesson.... The Excited Explorers and the
Hysterical Historians—a club. ... Checklist.

Identifying the talented child. ... Cultivating a capacity
for aesthetic response.... Expressing feelings through
the arts.... Creating self-portraits by cutting and
folding paper. ... Figure drawing with models. ... How
to make a diorama.... Suggestions for creating a pipe
cleaner city.... Using collage.... Making a research
mural.... The piper leads the way—a core curricu
lum.... The Michelangelo Ceiling Society—a club....
Checklist.

Finding the talented. ... Outdoor orbits—what to do
when role-playing the planets.... Some ways to build
an erosion model.... Planning an Insect Hunt....
Studying spiders.... How to create a miniature forest
floor.... Having a Science Fair—parent and teacher
involvement.... Creating a recipe from algae.... The
Mad Scientists' Club. ... Checklist.

Activities for Motivating and Teaching Bright Children

Challenging
the Verbally Bright

Chapter One

Children are not things that can be put into packages and labelled. They are so complex and have so many needs and talents. The verbally bright child is commonly bright in very many ways. We must seek out and nurture his other gifts too.

A child who has a high verbal intelligence needs different instruction from that of his average classmates. He needs shorter lessons, more complex tasks, more critical thinking, and more independence. Do not expect him to sit through a long class instruction period, as he might get too bored to be able to do the activity at all. Permit him to start ahead of the others. Allow him the freedom to work on his own for everything except very new and difficult class lessons. Have him keep a record system of progress charts to plot his own accomplishments. You will see a happy, motivated learner.

This chapter will help you to recognize the verbally bright child. It will suggest activities for challenging him: using humor, a limerick contest, planning puzzles, creating haiku, composing analogies, previewing for the class, preparing living biographies with shadow voices, and using a card catalogue in a new way. It will provide an interest inventory, sample literature lessons, and will show you how to help those who want to write. It will suggest procedures for initiating a special club for these pupils, and provide ideas for stimulating activities during their meetings.

Who Are They? How to Recognize Them

We may be able to identify the verbally bright child the easiest of all, because there are usually so many clues to guide us. The verbally gifted child usually shows his talent in speaking and reading at an early age. He uses a large vocabulary well in phrases and sentences, and he will continue to use an advanced vocabulary for his age with ease. He can see relationships. He likes puzzling questions and tries to give reasons for his answers. The truly gifted child is inner-directed, and very interested in his activities. He can become totally absorbed in a book. He needs no outside pressure, but finds pleasure in his intellectual occupations.

A child with a high verbal intelligence will score high on an IQ test. It is very important, however, that you know what test is used. The best test for any age group is one that has a high enough ceiling to screen out the gifted. For example, the California Test of Mental Maturity (Elementary) has a maximum IQ score of 136 for 14-year-olds. It would be unsuitable for that age group, but its ceiling of 157 for 12-year-olds would make this test suitable for 12-year-olds and younger children. The Stanford-Binet ceiling of 167 for 14-year-olds tells us that this test is good for children over 12.[1] An individual test is always more reliable than a group test.

Some very vivacious, talkative children with a great deal of self-confidence may give the impression of being brighter than they are. A quiet, shy child may be more gifted than the pushy talker. So, superficial observation is not enough. The *quality* of the child's speech may be a better indication than its quantity.

There is an obvious overlapping between the various talents. For instance, a child who has a talent in creative writing is also verbally talented, talented in the arts, and gifted with creativity.

Be cautious about identification of intelligence with children

---

[1] Robert F. DeHaan and Robert J. Havighurst, *Educating Gifted Children*. (Chicago, Illinois: The University of Chicago Press, 1961), pp. 43-44.

from deprived backgrounds, and use non-verbal intelligence tests. These children may have a high intelligence and a potential for verbal ability which is blocked and hidden by lack of models and lack of stimulation in their environment.

Using Humor

If your verbally bright pupils are not punsters, it is only because they haven't thought of it yet. A good sense of humor and a delight in puns seem to be characteristic of bright people.

If your pupils are unfamiliar with puns, introduce them to a few with a good laugh. Impress children with how old this form of humor is, as it goes back to Aristophanes, Cicero, and Shakespeare. Explain that a pun is a play upon words which have different meanings, but the same or similar sounds. Try to convince your pupils never to be embarrassed about making puns, as they are much more than silly jokes. They require good thinking — seeing relationships.

Your students will enjoy reading puns, discussing them, and later, writing some of their own. They will have to be very familiar with puns before they attempt this.

Allow children to discover for themselves that they're really working with the familiar *homonym*, only they're having more fun!

Many old, old jokes are based on puns.

What country does the cook use? (Greece)
What is it that stays hot in a refrigerator? (mustard)
Why is Sunday the strongest day? (because it isn't a weekday)

Bring some joke and pun books to class. One good book of puns is *Pun Fun*.[2]

Composing Limericks — A Contest

The Limerick Contest (for the entire class) can be as absurd as limericks themselves. Your students may decide that everyone

---

[2] Ennis Rees, *Pun Fun* (New York: Abelard-Schuman, 1965).

or no one wins. The main thing is that the children make an earnest attempt to write a real limerick in the accepted style. The students may have ridiculous content in their limericks, but they must take the form seriously. They will find this a challenging, delightful experience.

To begin with, enjoy many limericks together. Before pupils start to write limericks give many, many good examples. *The Big Book of Limericks (to laugh at)* is an excellent source.[3] These new limericks are very funny, and each one has a delightful and humorous illustration.

Another good book of limericks is *Laughable Limericks.*[4] It combines old and new limericks.

After the children have become very familiar with limericks, write one on the blackboard and ask about its form. Allow the children to discover that the first two lines rhyme with the last, and that lines three and four have a different rhyme. Help pupils to notice that the last line usually contains something unexpected or funny.

Analyze the limericks for their style. Point out the most contrived ones, and search for cleverness, wit, and originality. When everyone in your class has been steeped in limericks, declare the contest open to all and allow plenty of time and paper. Most of your verbally bright students will enter; but if you have one or two lazy ones, assign them the job of being a judge. This is a good large-group exercise in which your verbal pupils will probably put forth the most effort, but don't exclude anyone.

When you read the limericks aloud after the contest (no names), try to draw out constructive comments to show the group why some limericks are the best, and how some could be improved.

Planning Puzzles

Any kind of puzzle will be stimulating for the verbal child because he likes to think. His favorite kind will probably be puzzles made from words and letters.

---

³ Edward S. Mullins, *The Big Book of Limericks (to laugh at)* (New York: The Platt & Munk Co., Inc., 1969).

⁴ Sara and John E. Brewton (compilers), *Laughable Limericks* (New York: Thomas Y. Crowell Company, 1965).

Verbal ability is needed to compose effective anagrams. Explain that the word *anagram* comes from a Greek word which means "to transpose letters." Students will choose a word and try to rearrange its letters to make another word:

TIED

DIET

They can practice on longer or more difficult words, and then go on to phrases. It will be very absorbing for these children.

THING

NIGHT

DICTIONARY

A DIRTY COIN

Acrostics are also fun to write. They are words formed by the first letter of each line of a composition. For example:

<u>S</u>ometimes wintertime is fun.
<u>N</u>ot when the blizzards blow.
<u>O</u>nly when I'm skiing, and
<u>W</u>hen I glide and swoop below.[5]

Crossword puzzles are particularly enjoyable for the verbally bright because they're so good at them. Most adult puzzles have too many obscure (even for adults) references to be satisfying, so try to find some crossword puzzles designed for young people. Let them work many of them, with no help at first, as children will enjoy seeing how far they can go on their own. Then, before frustration sets in, allow the dictionary, and permit youngsters to help each other. It's important to them that they complete the puzzle, if possible.

After much practice with these puzzles, provide blanks for crossword puzzles. You can copy the blanks and duplicate them for pupils to compose their own puzzles. Also, suggest that some of your "word whizzes" make up their own blanks and puzzles. Children will work much harder on them than they do on their regular "work." Encourage pupils to extend their vocabularies and use new words if they can. Tell them that if they make the puzzles too easy they won't be able to "stump" their friends.

---

[5] Rosalind Minor Ashley.

Creating Beauty in Words — Haiku

All of your pupils will benefit from writing haiku, and most will be able to do it; but your verbally bright pupils will revel in it. They will be able to use language as an artist uses a delicate brush — with precision and beauty.

Try to help the children capture the essence of haiku, its condensed picture, the way it captures a scene — a season. The 17-syllable, 5-7-5 form is just a device, as the essense of haiku is simple loveliness. Give youngsters many examples of haiku:

The air is so still.
All life breathes hidden, afraid.
A wild storm is near.[6]

Help children to discover the recurring themes of the seasons, pairs of things in nature, and natural beauty. This may be their first experience with poetry that doesn't rhyme.

One lovely book of haiku is *Birds, Frogs, and Moonlight*.[7] It contains poetry translated from Japanese.

Janet Yearout, a teacher in a special program for the gifted, has created the following lesson for students of junior high age.[8] This lesson is planned to include experiences at these levels: cognitive, memory, convergent, divergent, and evaluation.

I. *Overall Purpose:* To increase the students' ability to express their ideas and feelings imaginatively and effectively.

II. *Today's Objective:* To introduce students to the reading and writing of haiku.

III. *General Procedure:* Viewing of pictures and listening to haiku will be used to interest students in the writing of haiku.

IV. *Background:* Students have engaged in various types of creative writing. Today's lesson is the first on poetry.

V. *Materials:* A. Harold G. Henderson, *An Introduction to Haiku*, Doubleday Anchor Books (Garden City, New York, 1958).

B. Several attractive magazine cutouts of unusual scenes from nature. (Haiku is often concerned with natural beauty and man's reaction to it.)

---

[6] Rosalind Minor Ashley.
[7] Sylvia Cassedy and Kunihiro Suetake (translators), *Birds, Frogs, and Moonlight* (Garden City, New York: Doubleday & Company, Inc., 1967).
[8] Janet Yearout, M.A., Enhanced Learning Program for Gifted, Pinellas County Schools, Clearwater, Florida.

VI. *Activities:*

A. *Motivation* — Students are shown a picture of an autumn scene and asked to name as many words as they can which describe the scene and their reaction to it. These words are recorded on the board.

B. *Activity* — Students are introduced to haiku by the reading of poems relating to autumn. They are told — this is how the poet reacted to a scene similar to the one you have just viewed. The class discusses the poems and their style. Class members are then asked to write haiku about the autumn scene, using the words on the blackboard. These poems are shared, if children wish to share them.

C. *Culminating Activity* — Several pictures are displayed as a stimulus for writing haiku. Pupils are free to use other ideas if they wish.

VII. *Follow-Up and Assignment:* Students may share their haiku with the class.

VIII. *Evaluation:*

A. Was the stimulus effective in arousing interest?

B. Did students understand the haiku form?

C. Did students enjoy the writing of haiku?

D. Did students listen as others read their poems to the class?

Using Analogies

> A glove is to a hand
> As a <u>shoe</u> is to a <u>(foot)</u>.
>
> A lamb is to a sheep
> As a <u>kitten</u> is to a <u>(cat)</u>.
>
> Bricks are to a wall
> As <u>shingles</u> are to a <u>(roof)</u>.

Analogies are much more than an interesting way of using language. They're a way of thinking — of seeing relationships between classes of things. Your verbally bright children will make a game of composing analogies once they are familiar with them.

Give pupils a few examples, and make sure they understand that the missing word must be related to its word *in the same way* that the last word in the first sentence is related to *its* word. Analyze the elements of some analogies. Point out that many of them involve parts of things, things related by size, things worn in the same way, etc. They can be simple and still be very satisfying to the children.

Class Previewers

Your very able children will enjoy acting as class previewers for filmstrips. Take the time to brief them fully on the subjects of present and future units of study for which they might find filmstrips. Discuss the level of difficulty they should look for, emphasizing that if the filmstrip is too difficult for them, they should not select it for the group.

Gifted pupils will also be able to do a good job of selecting room books from the library in subjects relative to units of study. In the process, they will delve into many books that they will read and enjoy.

Preparing Living Biographies — Shadow Voices

Biographies are especially appealing to bright children, both boys and girls. Some prefer to read about Presidents of the United States, others about inventors. These children tend to identify with the people whose lives they read about. They find these books fascinating because the people they were written about really lived.

A project that will be very exciting for your verbally bright elementary pupils will be to prepare living biographies with shadow voices. A group of four or five pupils will do this before or after school, each one working alone. Individuals will keep the identity of the rest of the group a secret. Each one will select a famous person, whisper the name to you, and do secret research on this person's life. When he knows as much as possible about his subject, he will use his notes to write a short monologue that will supposedly be written by the famous person. This first-person monologue will contain clues for his classmates to use to guess who the famous person is. The student will write two extra clues that will not be in the monologue to save for the class presentation. When the monologue is written, he will record it.

When four or five monologues are ready, advertise the living biographies with shadow voices. Do not identify any of the speakers or the subjects of their biographies. The class will enjoy this new kind of program.

Begin by allowing students to guess the names of the shadow

voices. As they are recognized, have the performers each take turns leading the group in discovering who his secret person is. The leader will replay the tape and allow guesses. If no one can guess after the clues on the tape, allow the leader to give one or two more clues. Then, if the audience still does not guess, go on to the next biography. If there is time at the end, replay the difficult biographies, and let the class try again. When your time is up, the leader may tell the secret names of all the biographies that have not been guessed.

How to Use a Card Catalogue to Motivate Wide Reading

Plan to enlarge your classroom library. It is very convenient for children to be able to browse among a wide selection of books in their own classroom.

When pupils order paperback books from some of the good, inexpensive book clubs, the classroom receives one book for every five ordered, if the class uses the company's weekly publication.[9] In this way, you can choose a selection to please most of the class. Try to get science, biography, humor, mystery stories, sports, history, etc.

Assign the responsibility of making a card catalogue to four or five of your verbally gifted pupils. If they need a little review on the card catalogue, send them in to the library to look at it. Perhaps the librarian can go over the system with them. They will probably return enthused over their assignment. Divide up the classroom books among the group, and have the pupils glue paper pockets inside the front covers to hold cards. Have the children make out a book card for the pocket of each book. The card should contain the author's last name and the title of the book.

You will also need an author card, a title card, and a subject card for each book for the card catalogue (Figure 1-1). The catalogue will list all books in three ways. It can be stored in a shoe box.

Use the Dewey Decimal System for classifying the books, with the numerals on the cards and on the spines of the books. Your librarian can give you the classification numbers.

---

[9] Arrow Books, Scholastic Book Services, Englewood Cliffs, New Jersey/Pleasanton, California.

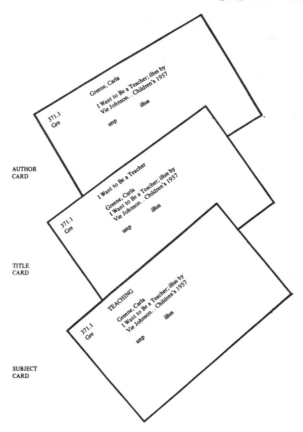

AUTHOR
CARD

TITLE
CARD

SUBJECT
CARD

Figure 1-1

A filmstrip that will be very useful to the children doing this project is *Using the Library — The Card Catalogue.*[10] It will show them how the cards are made out and how the card catalogue is used.

This card catalogue activity will contribute to the welfare of the class, as it will organize its library for finding and checking out books. Also, by handling and classifying the books, your bright students will become more aware of the variety of subjects

---

[10] *Using the Library — The Card Catalogue,* 9842C-S, Encyclopaedia Britannica Educational Corp. Film Library, 1822 Pickwick Ave., Glenview, Illinois 60025.

available in books, and will be tempted to vary their reading more. Even if they keep on reading the same kind of books, you will have exposed them to many different types of reading which they may turn to later. These children, if they are reading only fiction, will certainly become interested in a variety of subjects in their reading.

By having a card catalogue for your own class library, your pupils will have a better understanding of the organization of the larger library. They will also be able to use it more effectively.

Interest Inventories

> To engage successfully in the guidance of a gifted pupil's reading, the teacher requires information pertaining to the pupil's personal life. From interest inventories, clues may be obtained which will help the teacher understand pupils' attitudes, problems, and adjustment. Occasionally, such a study makes it clear that the teacher's major problem is to develop more varied or worthwhile patterns of interest. Activities and experiences (properly chosen) are needed by the gifted for enrichment and as a basis for the development of effective and meaningful reading. Despite the fact that the background of the typical gifted child is usually rich and varied, there are some who live in limited or impoverished environments and whose chief need is the extension of experience. Indeed, one of the major problems commonly encountered by the regular classroom teacher who has one or more gifted children in his group is the provision of such enrichment.[11]

A sample interest inventory follows. It can be used from the third through the eighth grades:

---

[11] Reprinted by permission of the publisher, from P.A. Witty, A.M. Freeland, E.H. Grotberg, *The Teaching of Reading: A Developmental Process* (Lexington, Mass.: D.C. Heath and Company, 1966) p. 347.

INTEREST INVENTORY

NAME _____ AGE_____
GRADE_____ SEX _____
What is your favorite hobby? _____
Any others? _____
When you have free time to do what you want, what do you like
to do? _____
What game do you like best? _____
Any others? _____
Do you have any pets? _____
What pets do you have?_____
Do you like to make things? _____
What things do you like to make? _____
What kind of movies do you like? _____
What are your two favorite television programs? _____
_____
What books have you enjoyed reading more than any others?
_____
What do you like to read about? Underline the names of these
things and add others.

animals   science   make-believe   knights of old
covered-wagon days   trains and planes   mysteries
everyday stories   biographies   funny things   sports

What person do you want to be like? (in real life or stories)
_____

If you could have three wishes come true about yourself, what
would they be?
1. _____
2. _____
3. _____

If you could have three wishes come true about school, what
would they be?
1. _____
2. _____
3. _____
What are your favorite subjects in school?_____
_____
What are your favorite sports? _____
_____
What kind of work would you like to do some day? _____
_____

Figure 1-2

More Sample Lessons

The following lessons by Janet Yearout are from a series that was specially planned for classes for the gifted in grades 1-3:[12]

I. *Overall Purpose:* To introduce students to stories, tales, and poems whose themes are concerned with values.

II. *Today's Objective:* To introduce students to a story where problems presented provide pupils with a chance to elaborate and modify it.

III. *General Procedure:* Procedure will be reading, drawing, and sharing work with the class.

IV. *Background:* All students in the class are anxious to respond, but this is often impossible. Today's lesson will allow each an individual response to the problems presented.

V. *Materials:* Lofting, Hugh. *Travels of Dr. Dolittle.* (New York: Random House, 1967). *Art Materials* — Heavy drawing paper cut and assembled to form a small book; crayons, Magic Markers.

VI. *Activities: Introductory Activity* — Explanation of lesson: Today in the story, Dr. Dolittle is presented with several problems. As we come to these problems in the story, I shall ask you to draw the way you might have suggested Dr. Dolittle solve the problem. When we are through, each one will have a book showing how he would have helped Dr. Dolittle in his travels. *Activity* — Read story, stopping to allow for student interpretation as the problems present themselves. *Culminating Activity* — Students will share the books they have created and discuss the solutions if time permits.

VII. *Follow-Up and Assignment:* If you have to make a decision this week or solve a problem, think of all the different ways you can go about finding a solution.

VIII. *Evaluation:* Did students enjoy the problem-solving approach? Were the responses original? Did they enjoy seeing each other's work? Were they able to compare and contrast the various solutions?

*   *   *   *   *

---

[12] Janet Yearout, M.A., Enhanced Learning Program for Gifted, Pinellas County Schools, Clearwater, Florida.

I. *Overall Purpose:* To introduce students to stories, tales, and poems whose themes are concerned with values.

II. *Today's Objective:* To introduce students to a story dealing with both victory and defeat; to allow students to compare the feelings of Ramu, an Indian boy, with their own.

III. *General Procedure:* Reading, discussion, and art activity.

IV. *Background:* Students are aware that each of the stories discussed deals with values and are quick to recognize and discuss them.

V. *Materials:* Gobhai, Mehlli. *Ramu and the Kite.* (Englewood Cliffs, New Jersey: Prentice-Hall, Inc., 1970). *Art Materials* — construction paper, crayons, Magic Markers, string.

VI. *Activities: Introductory Activity* — What do you think the story will be about? Do you think children in all countries enjoy similar toys and games? Why or why not? *Activity* — Reading the story, stopping to ask pertinent questions. *Discussion Following the Story* — How did Ramu feel after he won his first kite battle? Have you ever felt like that? Why wasn't Ramu ready to fight the white kite? How do you feel when you aren't ready? How did Ramu feel when he lost his kite? Have you ever felt like that? What was the silver kite trying to tell Ramu? Do you think Ramu will buy a new kite? *Culminating Activity* — Construction of a wind sock or mobile type kite.

VII. *Follow-Up and Assignment:* As you play games during the week, sometimes winning, sometimes losing, think about how you feel. Are your feelings similar to those of Ramu?

VIII. *Evaluation:* Were students able to identify with feelings of both victory and defeat? Were they able to recognize the symbols in the story? Was a tense atmosphere produced by this serious story? Did the art activity serve to reduce this tension?

*   *   *   *   *

I. *Overall Purpose:* To introduce students to stories, tales, and poems whose themes are concerned with values.

II. *Today's Objective:* To allow students to work in their particular interest, to provide manipulative activities for the younger children.

III. *General Procedure:* Centers of interest are arranged within the classroom — one with puzzles and picture arrangement cards, one with books, and one with records. Students may move freely among these centers.

IV. *Background:* The students seem to enjoy independent activities and activities which allow them to construct and manipulate objects. Today's lesson will capitalize on this interest.

V. *Materials:* Animal puzzles, people puzzles, books, records, picture arrangement cards.

VI. *Activities:* Class members work independently or in groups and the teacher is free to move among them. Those working with puzzles and picture arrangement cards will be encouraged to create stories using these materials as a stimulus.

VII. *Follow-Up and Assignment:* Students may bring their favorite books and records to share with the class.

VIII. *Evaluation:* Were the activities provided varied enough to interest all students? Did students move from one area to another, or were they preoccupied with one activity for the entire period? Did students who worked together display interest in the ideas of others? Did students cooperate with each other and share the materials willingly? Were those working with manipulative objects able to create stories using them? Did all students enjoy the lesson?

*   *   *   *   *

Wanting to Write

Many verbal children love to write and dream of becoming authors. Encouragement and opportunity to write are the best things you can provide.

This should start very early. A bright child in kindergarten must have opportunities to look at books from which he can learn something. He can help the teacher write names and signs, make little books and newspapers, and give puppet shows.

One middle-grade teacher initiated a class project when she was fortunate enough to obtain the donation of a room-size paper two-headed dragon from a local chain store. [13] Her class published a book called *The Adventures of Firecracker, a Two-Headed Dragon,* written and illustrated by the Creative Writers and Dragon Lovers of Room 12. The book had a "copyright" and a dedication. Each chapter was written by one pupil, inspired by

---

[13] Audrey Werner, Middlefork School, Sunset Ridge School District #29, Northfield, Illinois.

Firecracker's awesome presence on the ceiling. True, very few of us are lucky enough to come upon dragons — but we should be opportunists when it comes to bringing visual stimuli into our classrooms.

This same teacher had a resource person come to give a paper puppet show for her class. The stage was the back of a chair, and the settings were decorated paper sheets that flipped over the back of the chair. Most of the paper characters had string attached at the heads. The children in her class were so enthralled with the show that many of them paired up to write and produce their own paper puppet shows at home. They brought sets, characters, and original scripts, and were well-rehearsed. One child moved the characters while the other read the script, and then they switched parts. There were so many of these original productions that it was difficult to fit them all in, but everyone heartily enjoyed them.

Another creative teacher's class went from a study of the stars and the Zodiac to myths, fairy tales, and fables, and published books of stories by the 28 Authors Publishing Company. [14] Each pupil created a fine, completely bound book with all important parts.

One child wrote an illustrated fable, the text of which is reproduced below:[15]

PETEY Q'S GREED
by Kasia Stoloski

Once, a long time ago, there lived a family of monkeys. There were at least 20 families.

There was one family, and they had a little boy named Petey Q, and he was always getting into mischief because he loved candy. But his family was very poor so they did not have any candy for Petey Q. So Petey Q always stole candy from other monkeys.

One day his father came home yelling, "I found lots of candy," and Petey Q was so happy. His mother took a jar and filled it with candy, then she hid it so Petey Q could not get it.

---

[14] Margaret Goldman, Middlefork School, Sunset Ridge School District #29, Northfield, Illinois.
[15] Kasia Stoloski, Grade 3, 273 Thackeray Lane, Northfield, Illinois.

The next day Petey Q had eaten up all the candy. Then his mother let him have some of the candy she had saved, and when he stuck his hand in and tried to get his hand out, he couldn't! And then he began to cry. His mother said, "Let half of it go." But Petey Q said, "No" — and his hand remained stuck in the jar forever!

THE MORAL — Half is better than none.

THE END

Someday You'll Write is a guide to writing for young people aged 11 or older. [16] It explains how the writer chooses his subject, develops the narrative, keeps the reader interested — and also, how he disciplines himself.

Upper elementary and junior high students who use words well will be intrigued by a book called *What's Behind the WORD?* [17] It tells, in a very interesting way, the stories behind words we use all of the time. It delves into the backgrounds of such words as *sandwich, sabotage, clue, boycott, diaper, pretzel, ketchup, cockpit,* and many more.

Encourage your would-be authors to enlarge their already enormous vocabularies. If words are to be their trade (or their hobby), they cannot know enough of them.

A *Vocabulary Development Program* gives enrichment for verbally bright youngsters in an interesting way. [18] It consists of an album with two 33-1/3 rpm long-playing records. Each record is divided into eight bands, four bands on each side. On each band you will hear eight non-technical, useful, frequently encountered words. A Test/Review Book is included.

The Calm and Quiet Debating Society — a Club

Your verbally bright older students will enjoy a club of their

---

[16] Elizabeth Yates, *Someday You'll Write* (New York: E.P. Dutton & Co., Inc., 1962).

[17] Harold Longman, *What's Behind the WORD?* (New York: Coward-McCann, Inc., 1968).

[18] Nora Rotzoll and Ronald Mochel, *Vocabulary Development Program,* narrated by Jerry Kaufherr; produced by Vocab Incorporated, 1968. Scott, Foresman and Company, Glenview, Illinois.

own in which their talk is socially acceptable — on the agenda. Debating is a great skill and must be gone into thoroughly and done well. Your big talkers will argue and shout, but they will learn from it. Do not attempt debates for able students any sooner than junior high school.

Use a good reference to help you. Some helps for debaters can be found in *The First Book of How to Make a Speech* [19] and in *The World Book Encyclopedia.* [20]

Have each club member read all about the subject and discuss it before the club attempts a debate. Their topic should be one of general interest, and one that can be defended in two ways.

Debating is only one activity that this club can engage in. Middle- and upper-grade verbal youngsters may enjoy a writing project in which they attempt to write simple mystery stories. Have the children read many mystery stories first. They can begin with *Eight Mystery Stories* and analyze the clues and how the mysteries were solved. [21] The members may never learn how to write a good mystery story, but they will end up with a hearty appreciation for the skill that it takes to write one.

Another good activity for this club is to team up with a club for children who are socially bright and help them with their election campaigns for class offices. The verbal group can write advertising and help with ideas for speeches.

Some meetings can be devoted to word games and puzzles. "Scrabble® for Juniors," a spelling and word game, can be a challenging experience. [22] Game I, played on the front side of the board, has as its object: to spell out all interlocking words that are printed on the board, by covering each letter with a matching letter tile, covering the letters of each word in order. Young players in the six- to 12-year age group will improve their spelling and knowledge of words by playing Game I. After that, they can play the more advanced Game II. Anagrams can also be a good meeting activity.

------

[19] David Guy Powers, *The First Book of How to Make a Speech* (New York: Franklin Watts, Inc., 1963).

[20] "Debate," *The World Book Encyclopedia* (1970), IV, 1896-98.

[21] Mike Neigoff, *Eight Mystery Stories* (Glenview, Illinois: Scott, Foresman and Company, 1971).

[22] Selchow & Righter Company, Bay Shore, New York, for Production and Marketing Company, edition three, 1968.

Some of the meetings can be devoted to writing and sharing letters for World Pen Pals. This club can team up for the activity with the club for children who have aptitude in social studies. Not only will your students get letter-writing practice, but some of the older ones will get opportunities to correspond in French, German, Spanish, or Portuguese. See Chapter Four for the section on World Pen Pals.

CHECKLIST

Provide verbally bright children with shorter lessons, more complex tasks, more critical thinking, and more independence than other pupils.

Try to identify children with verbal gifts by watching for these things: They use a large vocabulary *well* in speaking and reading at an early age. They score high on IQ tests.

Use non-verbal intelligence tests for children from deprived backgrounds.

Use puns, limericks, anagrams, acrostics, and crossword puzzles as valuable activities.

Teach haiku and analogies: both are activities that require deep thinking.

Plan for verbally bright youngsters to enjoy and benefit from previewing filmstrips and books for the class.

Use the preparation and presentation of living biographies with shadow voices, which will require research, planning, and critical thinking.

Have pupils prepare a card catalogue for your room library to motivate reading.

Try interest inventories, to help you extend the experiences of your pupils.

Use literature with gifted pupils for problem-solving experiences and opportunities to understand their own and others' feelings.

Encourage creative writing with visual and auditory stimuli.

Extend pupils' vocabularies with records and challenging practice.

Help pupils initiate and maintain a club of their own in which they enjoy debating, writing, puzzles, games, and letter writing to Pen Pals.

Individualizing with Your Own Programmed Material

Chapter Two

Many people think that programmed teaching material must be very complex and difficult to work with. Its content can be as simple or as advanced as you wish. However, by its very nature, programmed material must be simple in form.

What is commonly called *programmed instruction* is automatic self-teaching of material via a *program*. A *program* is a body of knowledge or information organized into a series of sequential concepts for self-instructional purposes. Continuous and immediate evaluation of the student's progress is provided. The program is presented in a device or format that controls and directs the student's access through the material, and that demands the student's commitment.

A sample scrambled programmed section is provided for you in Chapter Three. It teaches a very few language concepts for advanced third grade children. The instruction consists of a tutorial interaction between two fantasy story characters: a pupil and his teacher. It is written in informal dialogue in order to be of maximum interest to the child.

In this chapter, you will have samples of a Content Outline, Behavorial Instructional Objectives, a Pre-Test — Post-Test, and a Bubble Diagram. You will receive help in planning and writing your own programmed teaching booklet. You will begin by selecting one main concept or skill that you wish to teach. You will get suggestions for writing Instructional Objectives that are *behavioral*, which can be tested. You'll learn how to use a Pre-Test — Post-Test. This will help you to know whether the pupil *needs* to study the concept. Perhaps he knows it already. Also, in case he doesn't know it, the test tells you whether or not he has learned it after using the booklet. You will learn how to construct a Bubble Diagram, which is nothing more than a plan for organizing your booklet's pages in a *scrambled* or random manner. When you see how easy it is to plan and write a programmed booklet of your own, you will be eager to try it. You may also wish to use the sample section, which can be made into a booklet, and adapt it for your own class.

A Simple Plan of Action

Your plan will begin with what you wish to teach. You will probably choose a single main concept or skill, with a few related ideas.

The two main systems of programming are *linear programming* and *intrinsic programming*. A *linear program* has a single, pre-determined series of steps to a goal, and it goes in a straight line. This type is often used in a machine, and it may be set up so that errors may be reviewed at the end of the set sequence. Programmed textbooks of this type lead from familiar concepts to new materials, from one page to the next. A short lesson is given, and then a question is asked. Responses are usually constructed from an unlimited number of alternatives.

Intrinsic programming also has material that leads from the familiar to the new. It is organized into a series of sequential concepts, each lesson followed by appropriate multiple-choice questions used to evaluate and insure the student's understanding of the material. The student's choice of an answer to a multiple-choice question can be used diagnostically. Intrinsic programming has what is called *branching*, because selection of the next lesson to be presented depends on the response given in the current lesson.

In intrinsic booklets, each program step gives the student a short paragraph of material to read. This unit of material is followed by a multiple-choice question. Each answer alternative has a page number beside it. The student's answer choice determines directly and automatically what material he will see next. He chooses an answer and turns to the page whose number is given for that answer. If he selects the correct answer to the question, he is automatically presented with the next new paragraph of material and the next question. If he chooses an incorrect answer, he is automatically presented with material written specifically to correct the particular error he has made. In very simple cases, he may be told why his answer is incorrect, and be directed to the original presentation to have a second try at the original question. He may also be directed to instructional material covering the question he missed, with discussion and questions. The old material may be retaught in a new way in smaller steps or with a different approach. He will not come to the next unit of new material until he has chosen, or has been helped to choose, the correct answer.

The student who chooses one incorrect alternative is usually directed to other material from that of a different incorrect answer. The corrective expository material is appropriate to that response and to the pupil's needs. These booklets can also direct pupils to other media, if necessary or desirable.

The pages of the lessons are randomly arranged. The page numbers given with the answer choices are not consecutive or in any other obvious order. The student cannot ignore a question and routinely pass to the next page of material. He must select one answer and go on to the page he is directed to. His next page is the one given with his answer choice, not the sequentially numbered next page. This method, by directing the learner to a new page that can be located *anywhere* in the book, can control the child's natural curiosity about looking ahead. The pupil *must* follow his own lessons that are planned for his needs. This type of booklet's pages are mixed up in order, so the type of material is called *scrambled.*

This scrambled, intrinsic material automatically adapts to individual differences among students. It makes them active, tells them what they are expected to learn, and keeps them informed of their progress.

An excellent, detailed manual on intrinsic programmed material is *A Writer's Guide: Techniques in Intrinsic Programming.*[1] This book teaches the programmed method in depth, for booklets and for teaching machines. It is based on extensive research in automated technical training.

This would be a good time for you to skim the sample section in the next chapter, just to get familiar with it. This sample is written in the intrinsic, scrambled form.

As a plan for your booklet, you will need to write a short list, or Content Outline, telling the concept or skill that you wish to teach, some related ideas, and all testable learning expected. A sample Content Outline for the sample section follows. It includes everything that is taught and questioned in the programmed booklet.

CONTENT OUTLINE

1. The booklet combines elements of storybooks, textbooks, and guessing games.
2. The pupil needs to know what a *subject* is because he uses subjects in every simple sentence he writes.
3. Some sentences are made up of words that make sense, but the *order* of the words in the sentences make them nonsense sentences.
4. A subject can be found at the beginning of a simple sentence.
5. A subject tells us who or what does something in a sentence, or who or what the sentence is about.

Figure 2-1

Along with your Content Outline, you will need to decide on your goals for the child as he works on the booklet. These will have to be behaviors that can be tested — not vague, general objectives.

---

[1] Richard E. Walther, Ed. D. and Norman A. Crowder, *A Writer's Guide: Techniques in Intrinsic Programming,* U.S. Industries, Inc., Educational Science Division, 12345 New Columbia Pike, Silver Spring, Maryland, 1965.

Once your plans have been made and jotted down, you are ready to begin. It will be useful for you to read the sample booklet section carefully now. You will find it in Chapter Three. Then you will want to return to this next section to begin work on your Behavioral Instructional Objectives.

Suggestions for Writing Behavioral Instructional Objectives That Work for You

You may wonder why it's necessary to take time to write out objectives, because it's obvious that your objective is for the pupil to learn the concept or skill you're trying to teach.

The reason why the objectives have to be spelled out in behavioral terms is that you will need them as the basis for writing your vital Pre-Test — Post-Test. These objectives must work for you. Only with real ones can you find out whether a pupil needs the booklet or whether it would be a waste of his time to work on it. With Behavorial Instructional Objectives, you can write a test that will measure change in learning after the booklet is completed. You will base your objectives on your Content Outline.

A color filmstrip called "Instructional Objectives" will be very valuable to you, if you can view it.[2] It is extremely well done, and you will be able to write good objectives after you've seen it.

The first sample objective for the sample booklet section is:

The pupil is able to select answers that show awareness of the function of the book he is using.

As you will notice later, this first objective is not considered important enough to be the basis of a question in the Pre-Test — Post-Test. However, all of the other objectives are used for the test.

This objective is included because it *is* important that the pupil know that he can expect to learn something from the book. Since its colloquial approach may mislead him, an objective of this

---

[2] W. James Popham, "Instructional Objectives," Vimcet Associates, Los Angeles, California, 1966.

kind should begin your first booklet, but if you write a series, you won't need it later. Notice the underlined words. They show an observable *action* that the child can perform. Achievement of this goal can be tested by his answer to the question on Page 1 of the sample booklet section.

The second sample objective is:

> The pupil is able to select answers that tell why he needs to know what a *subject* is.

This objective is needed as it makes the concept important to the learner.

The third sample objective is:

> The pupil is able to select answers that make sense, from a group of nonsense answers in incorrect word order.

This objective is needed to show the pupil that he really knows what a simple English sentence is, and that he can choose a real English sentence from a group of English words in nonsense or incorrect order. This is necessary before we can teach how a *subject* functions in a sentence.

Notice that the objective does *not* say this:

> The pupil knows that English sentences are written in a special order that we're used to.

This way of saying it would be stating the concept correctly, but because the word *know* is not measurable, we must avoid it. The behavior *to select answers* can be tested and is therefore used.

In a classroom discussion situation, a behaviorally stated Instructional Objective for the same concept could also be this:

> The pupil is able to select and tell which sentence makes sense from a group of nonsense answers in incorrect word order.

You might also substitute the word *write* for *tell* in the case of a written exercise or test.

The main point is that the objective be stated using an action that can be observed or measured in some way. Avoid such vague words as: *know, become familiar with, believe, understand, comprehend, appreciate, enjoy, like,* etc.

We may think that we can observe when a pupil understands or likes something, but we cannot be sure unless we can test it. (He might be smiling to himself about his birthday party on Saturday.)

Use observable behaviors such as: *select answers, construct, solve, describe, match, write, identify, name aloud, circle the names, list in writing, tell, record, point out, draw a diagram of,* etc.

If you will read the sample Behavioral Instructional Objectives that follow, you will notice that all of the objectives begin in the same way:

The pupil is able <u>to select answers</u> that . . .

Since all of the intrinsic programmed booklets are based on multiple-choice questions with answers, this is the only possible way to begin your objectives.

BEHAVIORAL INSTRUCTIONAL OBJECTIVES
The pupil is able <u>to select answers</u> that:

show awareness of the function of the book he is using;
tell why he needs to know what a *subject* is;
make sense, from a group of nonsense answers in incorrect word order;
show a missing first part of a sentence;
show a missing subject from a sentence;
show where a subject is found in a simple sentence;
tell what the subject does in a sentence;
identify a subject in a sentence.

Figure 2-2

So, you see how very simple it is to write correctly stated objectives for intrinsic programmed booklets:

(1) You begin by saying: "The pupil is *able to select answers* that . . ."

(2) You include *every* important concept that the booklet teaches, using your Content Outline.

(3) You make your objectives clear and direct, and avoid excess words.

One of the most unique books I have ever read is *Preparing Instructional Objectives*, a book written in the intrinsic scrambled form.[3] It teaches you not only how to write excellent Behavioral Instructional Objectives, but its humorous style also gives you much reading pleasure.

Educational objectives can vary in their difficulty for the learner, and in their value to him. A *Taxonomy of Educational Objectives* has been developed, which begins at the bottom level with recall of memorized facts and rises through comprehension, application, analysis, and synthesis, up to the top level — evaluation (or judgment).[4] You will find this book very useful in checking to see whether you are requiring pupils to think or just recall memorized facts. You will need some objectives of each kind, with emphasis on the critical thinking of analysis, synthesis, and evaluation.

Sample Pre-Test and Post-Test

Just as you used your Content Outline to write your Behavioral Instructional Objectives, you can now use your objectives to write your Pre-Test — Post-Test.

Write at least one test item for each objective, with this exception: awareness of the function of the programmed booklet.

The test is called Pre-Test — Post-Test because it can be used for both purposes, as long as you do not show the marked Pre-Test to the pupil. If you do, he might memorize the questions and answers without real understanding. Have the learner give you his completed Pre-Test, mark it, keep it, and let him know whether he is to do the booklet. If he does not know most of the answers, give him the booklet. When he has completed it, give the child a fresh copy of the test, and have him take it again. After marking the Post-Test *with* the pupil, give the marked test back to him so that he can find out how he did, and also so he can learn the correct answers for the questions he missed.

---

[3] Robert F. Mager, *Preparing Instructional Objectives* (Palo Alto, California: Fearon Publishers, 1962).

[4] Benjamin S. Bloom and others, (ed.), *Taxonomy of Educational Objectives, Handbook I, Cognitive Domain* (New York: Longmans, Green and Co., 1956).

If the child misses more than one answer on the Post-Test, direct him to the other media which teach the same concept. This is best placed on the last numbered page of the booklet. (See page 34 in the sample booklet section). It is not usually productive to repeat the booklet.

The test can be written with three or more answers to the questions. Never write only two answers, as this would increase the chance of guessing. While guessing may always be involved, a child has to do some thinking when he has three or more choices.

It is suggested that most of the test questions have four answers for primary pupils. Older children need five or more answer choices.

The sample Pre-Test — Post-Test for the sample programmed booklet is given below.

PRE-TEST — POST-TEST

DIRECTIONS: WRITE AN X̲ ON THE LINE BEFORE
THE ANSWER YOU CHOOSE.

1.   Choose the sentence that has the first part missing.
_____(a)   The house was made_____ brick.
_____(b)   The house was made of ___ .
_X_(c)   ___ _____was made of brick.
_____(d)   I don't know.

2.   You need to know what a subject is because . . .
_____(a)   I don't know.
_____(b)   they're made up of the most important words in the sentence.
_____(c)   you get the whole meaning from it.
_X_(d)   you use subjects whenever you speak and write.

3.   Choose the real sentence from the following.
_____(a)   Plane the made noise much so that I hear couldn't.
_X_(b)   The plane made so much noise that I couldn't hear.
_____(c)   The plane so couldn't much noise that made hear I.
_____(d)   I don't know.

4.   In a simple sentence, a *subject* can be found . . .

____(a)   near the end.

____(b)   anywhere in the sentence.

____(c)   I don't know.

_X_(d)   in the beginning.

5.   Choose the sentence that has a missing *subject.*

____(a)   The rain ___ stopped.

____(b)   The __ has stopped.

_X_(c)   __ ___ has stopped.

____(d)   I don't know.

6.   In a simple sentence, a *subject* . . .

____(a)   I don't know.

____(b)   does the same job as a period.

_X_(c)   Tells who or what the sentence is about.

____(d)   Tells what is happening or what the person is doing.

7.   Choose the sentence which has only its *subject* underlined.

____(a)   Girls <u>like</u> to play with dolls.

____(b)   Girls like <u>to</u> <u>play</u> with dolls.

____(c)   <u>Girls</u> like to play with <u>dolls.</u>

_X_(d)   <u>Girls</u> like to play with dolls.

____(e)   <u>Girls</u> <u>like</u> <u>to</u> play with dolls.

Figure 2-3

It is good to include "I don't know" as one answer choice, as it relieves the child's tensions if he doesn't know. He then feels that it is acceptable not to know, and he is less inclined to guess.

If you have too few questions on your test, a couple of lucky guesses can make the test unreliable and invalid. If you have only one or two concepts and objectives, be sure to write about three test questions for each objective, or you will not have a reliable, valid test.

Plan and check your test. It must be short enough so that the student can complete it comfortably within the time allotted. Prepare the answer key before the test is duplicated so that the correct responses can be randomly keyed. Also, be sure to proofread for errors before the student gets the test, and see that the *errors are corrected.* Writing good test questions is difficult, and you may want to consult one of the fine books that have been written on the subject.[5]

Each multiple-choice item has two parts. These are: (1) The *stem,* or beginning part of the question. This can be a direct question or an incomplete statement. (2) The *alternatives,* or answers. These can be words, clauses, sentences, numerals, pictures, graphs, diagrams, etc.

The list below gives you some clues on the most important things you must remember when you write any multiple-choice question for your booklet or test:[6]

1.   Keep the reading difficulty low (unless you are measuring reading or verbal skills).

2.   Avoid inter-dependent items.

3.   Be sure one item does not provide clues to another.

4.   Make the correct answer vary randomly among the choices in a set of items.

5.   Compare your objective and your test item to make sure that the item requires the performance of a task *critical* to the attainment of the objective.

6.   The *stem,* or beginning part of the question, must have only *one* question or problem.

7.   The stem must be definite, not vaguely worded.

8.   The stem must ask an important question. Avoid trivia.

9.   State your question or problem in positive terms. If it is necessary to use a negative, avoid confusion by capitalizing it (<u>NOT</u>, UNlikely, <u>EXCEPT</u>).

10. If the stem is written as an incomplete statement, have it contain as much of the problem as possible.

11. Keep your alternatives, or answers, brief.

12. Avoid wordiness in the stem.

---

[5] Max D. Engelhart, *Improving Classroom Testing,* What Research Says to the Teacher Series (Washington, D.C.: Association of Classroom Teachers of the NEA, 1964), 25¢.

[6] Les Brown, Georgia Brooks, Patricia J. Cocks, and Mildred E. Kersh, *An Operational Guide for Teacher Workshops,* Evaluation for Individualized Instruction, A Title III ESEA Project, 1400 W. Maple Avenue, Downers Grove, Illinois 60515.

13. Your alternatives must have only *one* best or correct answer or completion to the question.

14. The incorrect alternatives must not be absurd (unless you are specifically testing to see if pupils can differentiate absurdity or nonsense). Humor is fine, but absurdity clues the pupil to the fact that the answer is incorrect.

15. Avoid using one "trick" word in an otherwise correct response, just to catch the pupil.

16. The alternatives must be grammatically consistent with the stem. Each answer should be tested with the stem to insure that it makes a real sentence.   ·

17. Make all of your alternatives plausible The incorrect answers should tempt pupils who have incomplete or superficial knowledge of the concept.

18. Write your alternatives with similar grammatical construction, length, and degree of precision. A long, detailed alternative with three short ones can clue the answer.

19. Laws, principles, and generalizations of all kinds should be restated in words other than those used in actual instruction, to avoid testing verbal memory rather than comprehension.

How to Use the Sample Section for Your Own Needs

This type of programmed booklet will be very useful in any type of classroom. It is desperately needed by pupils in non-graded schools in classes with multi-age groupings, in which the teachers use a variety of textbook series and media because of the many levels at which individuals are working.

If you write a series of booklets for different levels, the cartoon student's age and experiences would vary with the level of the booklet's readers. The characters' personalities and distinguishing characteristics would remain the same. The writing style of the series would be informal and colloquial.

You may wish to use the dialogue style with the two characters, and write your own teaching material for a different subject, or for other concepts.

You may choose to write a programmed booklet without a storybook character and teacher. You can teach your material directly, addressing the pupil. If you want an instructional booklet without the dialogue, you can use the sample booklet as your guide and skip the conversation. It will make your booklet shorter, but it will still do the job.

Your Content Outline gives you the material that you are to teach. Use the outline to organize your teaching material, placing all the teaching points on a topic together. Include all material that is needed to fulfill the objectives, unless the student is assumed to know it.

You should have one right-answer page for every teaching point in the Content Outline.

Be sure to define each term and concept the first time they are used. Arrange your material in a logical order. This is usually from the simple, the known, and concrete concepts to the complex, the unknown, and abstract concepts. There are many exceptions to this, so the only rule is to follow the order that will best teach the student. Use small steps, with only one new fact on a page, using frequent repetition.

At the start of the book, you will probably want to go directly from an incorrect answer's reteaching page to the next question. This will give the child a feeling of success and progress, and avoid frustration.

By the end of the booklet, if the pupil is giving incorrect answers, extra practice pages are needed, and can easily be inserted before you lead him on.

Please notice Page 2 in the sample booklet. It is not illustrated on the Bubble Diagram (Figure 2-4, p. 53), as no page leads to it. No answer to a question on any page will direct the pupil to Page 2. He can reach it only by turning the pages consecutively, as in a traditional book. Page 2 reminds the learner that he must follow the rules or get lost. If you want to have a warning page for the pupil to follow the rules, have it on Page 2, the logical place where a child will turn if he's breaking the rules.

Try not to write multiple-choice questions with the same wording as the Pre-Test — Post-Test, even though they will, of course, ask about the same concepts. Look for a fresh approach.

One reading expert gives her opinion on readability formulas for predicting the grade level of your reading materials:

Much enthusiasm has been shown by educators and publishers in the utilization of reading formulas as predictors of the readability of materials. Readability is not an easily identified concept. It is a complex function of many factors that exert an influence upon a given reader; e.g., a child's previous experience, a child's interest in the subject matter he is reading, as well as the literary form and the author's style, in which presumably unfamiliar words are couched. A readability formula is not definitive. It is a statistical device dependent upon the interaction of a number of factors to measure the readability of passages, not the comprehension difficulties of individual words and sentences. A formula erroneously assumes that any correlation observed between two variables (e.g., word length and sentence length) must always exist. The impact of style, contents, or literary quality upon interest is not reflected. If properly used, a readability formula can serve as a preliminary short cut to ascertaining the difficulty of written materials. In the final analysis, what is readable depends not so much on the material to be read, but on the selection of something written within the range of the conceptual ability and experience of the person doing the reading.[7]

If you are writing your booklet for children with reading difficulties, or those younger than the bright third-graders for whom this sample booklet was written, you can adapt the sample by shortening and simplifying the sentences, shortening the lessons, and screening the vocabulary for difficult or ambiguous words. Have your character the same age as your pupils, or a bit older. Use four choices for your answers for the very young children, and include "I don't know" as one. Keep in mind that even for gifted children, you may not want to present certain concepts too early.

If you would like to write a booklet for children older than those for whom the sample was written, you can still use the sample booklet as a guide for style. Increase the amount and complexity of the content, and be sure to make your character

---

[7] Ruth Ann Hodnett, Research Specialist and Consultant in Reading, Clarendon Hills, Illinois.

older. Write at least five answer choices for your questions, with an "I don't know" as one answer.

Even though we can tell you that the sample plan for a booklet would be effective for most above-average third graders, you will have to use your judgment and the Pre-Test to help you decide on the suitability of your material. The two main criteria are whether the concept is appropriate for the child and whether the reading level is suitable.

Write your questions for the maximum amount of critical thinking and the least amount of recall or guessing. The pupil is not usually encouraged to guess at an answer, except on a question like the one on Page 1, where he could not possibly know the answer yet.

The first page of your booklet should be an odd-numbered page so that it will appear on the right-hand side of the open book.

In preparing the material, you can use the following code on each page to identify your material:

RA — Right answer page

WA — Wrong answer page

SS — Sub-sequence (for extra remedial material)

Give the pages a temporary sequential numbering until you do your scrambling.

You can prepare your own fine auxiliary material by tape recording the reteaching of the concept. On the last page of the booklet, list as many different ways of reteaching the concept as you can. If the child learns best in another modality, or if he has reading or emotional difficulties, it is necessary to use other types of materials. He may work well with the programmed booklets later in his school progress.

When you finish writing your booklet, check it to make sure that you have taught and questioned each concept on the Content Outline. Read through your Behavioral Instructional Objectives to see that they cover the Content Outline. Check your test to see that you have adequately tested for every objective.

If you use the simple procedure given here, the booklet will practically write itself. The main thing is to have fun with your writing — because if you do, your pupils will too — and they'll find it exciting to see what comes next.

How to Scramble an Intrinsic Programmed Booklet — a Bubble Diagram

A bubble diagram can be as simple or as complicated as the programmed booklet it represents.

The diagram in Figure 2-4 represents a very simple intrinsic scrambled booklet. Each numbered circle, or bubble, symbolizes a page in the booklet. The circles with very dark edges stand for the pages that the pupil is first directed to when he has chosen the correct answer.

The first set of bubbles on the sample diagram represents a problem or question on Page 1. Incorrect or incomplete answers to the problem lead the pupil to either Pages 3, 6, or 9. The best, most complete answer leads him to Page 4, which has a circle with a dark edge on the diagram.

Some pages direct the learner to other pages, but they have no questions. This is done either to keep each page a complete unit or because there is too much material for one page. Page 4 praises the pupil for answering correctly and directs him to Page 5. Pages 3, 6, and 9 tell the pupil that he did well, but that his answer is incomplete. They each discuss different things, tell him the missing parts, and then direct him to Page 5.

Page 5 introduces the booklet by discussing its form and its main concept. Then it directs the pupil to Page 7, where he finds his next question.

The sample diagram proceeds simply in this manner. The incorrect answer leading to Page 8 directs the pupil back to Page 7. There is no extra branching for remedial help until Page 27. This incorrect answer at a late stage in the booklet indicates a need for extra practice, which is given on Page 29. If the pupil can now select a sentence with a missing subject, he is directed to Page 30, which praises him, reviews the concept, and leads him to the next question on Page 31. If the child still does not understand the concept, this is demonstrated by either of the two incorrect answers that lead him to Page 25. Page 25 reteaches the location and function of a subject in a simple sentence. It then directs the

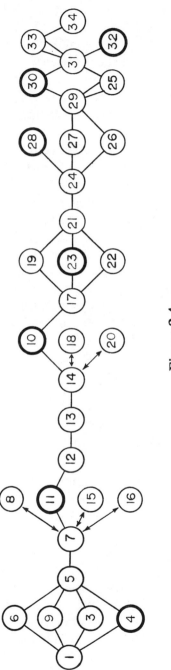

Figure 2-4

pupil to Page 31, which practices the concept and gives the last question. The correct answer to this takes him to Page 32, which ends the book for this pupil, just as Page 28 ended the book for pupils who were doing very well. Incorrect responses to the question on Page 31 lead the learner to Page 33 and then to Page 34, which branches him to auxiliary instruction in other media, such as filmstrips, films, overhead visuals, dittomasters, practice sheets, tapes, or records that might be more suitable to his learning style.

Plan your own booklet with your own Bubble Diagram. To begin with, figure out how many pages you will have in your booklet. Have a Pagination Check Sheet, which lists every numeral from 1 to the top number of pages in your booklet. Draw one bubble on your diagram for a lesson-and-question page. Write its page number on it. Begin with Page 1. Then draw lines from it to four other bubbles (if you have four alternatives). Write the page number of each alternative in each of these bubbles, giving a dark edge to the circle of the page number representing a page led to from the correct answer. As you number a page in the upper right-hand corner, and enter the numeral in a bubble, cross out the numeral on your Check Sheet. The remaining numbers are ready to work with and you will not get confused. Continue until all the pages are accounted for, except perhaps Page 2, your warning page.

You may follow the sample Bubble Diagram if you wish, rather than make up a new one. However, your material may cause you to adapt it somewhat. It doesn't matter in what order you mix the pages, as long as they're scrambled. Go back and forth in the booklet so that the pupil cannot tell what is coming next. You will use all the pages. Remember to darken the edge of the circle that represents the page a pupil turns to directly after a correct answer.

Once you've made the beginning of the Bubble Diagram, it will be fun for you to construct the branching for extra practice pages after incorrect answers. Just remember that you must either direct the pupil to another question; to extra practice and then a question; or to auxiliary material in other media.

So, like the booklet, the Bubble Diagram can be as simple or as complex as you wish to make it. You will probably want to start out very simply.

Arrange your booklet's pages numerically. The scrambling will follow the diagram. Your answer pages will be randomly distributed throughout the booklet.

Make sure that you check each question and answer to see that the answers are on the pages that the learner is directed to, and that the lessons and answers are keyed correctly, following the Bubble Diagram.

You will probably want to keep a simple chart for each pupil who is working on programmed material. It could include his name, the title of each booklet worked on, and his Pre-Test — Post-Test scores. If a Pre-Test score shows that a booklet for a specific concept is not needed, it would be checked off on the chart and skipped. When you grade the Post-Test with the child, enter his score and check off the booklet as completed.

You can duplicate each page of your booklet, making as many booklets as you need. Now that you have a style to follow, you can use it for a series on the same subject, and for many other subjects. Vary your Bubble Diagrams so that pupils cannot follow any remembered order of pages.

It is obvious that the programmed booklets would be useful and delightful to *all* children. However, it is the bright ones who need them so desperately. With programmed learning materials, nothing could stand in their way. They could progress as individuals and learn at their own speed.

Districts might profit by forming workshop groups to write programmed materials for all teachers. This could save much time and effort on the part of individual teachers. Teachers who write these booklets on their own could save time by sharing them with other teachers, each writing one series in her own best field. This material can be used again and again, giving truly individualized instruction.

CHECKLIST

Programmed instruction is automatic self-teaching of material via a *program*.

A *program* is a body of knowledge or information organized into a series of sequential concepts.

The two main systems of programming are *linear* and *intrinsic.*

A *linear* program has a single, pre-determined series of steps to a goal, each lesson with constructed answers to questions. Linear textbooks go from one page to the next.

An *intrinsic* program is organized into a series of sequential concepts, each followed by multiple-choice questions.

The *branching* of intrinsic programs selects the next lesson for the learner based on the response given in the current lesson.

Reteaching material in intrinsic programs is specific for the type of error made, individualizing each lesson.

Intrinsic programs are *scrambled* — the pages are organized in random order.

With scrambled page order, the learner must follow the program, do each lesson, and answer each question.

A Content Outline lists the concept or skill you wish to teach in a booklet, with some related ideas. It is a plan for the book.

You will need a list of Instructional Objectives based on the Content Outline.

Behavioral Instructional Objectives are observable and measurable and can be tested, so they work for you in determining the child's needs and progress.

Avoid using these verbs in your objectives, as they are not behavioral and cannot be observed or tested: *know, become familiar with, believe, understand, comprehend, appreciate, enjoy, like,* etc.

Use these words for objectives: *select answers, construct, solve, describe, match, write, identify, name aloud, circle the names, list in writing, tell, record, point out, draw a diagram of,* etc.

Begin Instructional Objectives for intrinsic programmed booklets with: *The pupil is able to select answers that . . .*

Vary your objectives, using recall of facts, comprehension, application, analysis, synthesis, and evaluation.

Expect all kinds of thinking behavior, with emphasis on the higher kinds of critical thinking.

Use your Instructional Objectives as the basis for your Pre-Test — Post-Test.

Use the same Pre-Test — Post-Test for both purposes, but do not mark it *with* the pupil until he has completed the booklet and Post-Test.

Skip the booklet if the child misses one or no answers on the Pre-Test.

Direct the child who misses more than one answer on the Post-Test to the recommended media on the last page of the booklet.

Write questions with four answers for primary level pupils. Never have only two answers. If you include an "I don't know" answer, have four or more answers.

Write questions with five or more answers for older students.

Have at *least* one test question for each objective. If you have only one or two objectives, write extra test questions for each one, to keep your test reliable and valid.

Write each multiple-choice item in two parts: a *stem*, or beginning, and *alternatives*, or answers.

Use these clues for writing good multiple-choice items:
> Keep the reading difficulty low.
> Avoid inter-dependent items.
> Be sure one item does not provide cues to another.
> Vary the correct answer randomly among the choices in a set of items.
> Have your test item require performance of a task *critical* to the attainment of the objective.
> Give the stem only one question or problem.
> Have the stem definite, and not vaguely worded.
> Have the stem ask an important question.
> State your question or problem in positive terms, if possible.
> Have the stem contain as much of the problem as possible if it is written as an incomplete statement.
> Keep your alternatives brief.
> Avoid wordiness in the stem and the alternatives.
> Write the alternatives so that you have only *one* best or correct answer or completion to the question.
> Plan incorrect alternatives that are not absurd, unless you are

specifically testing for the pupils' ability to differentiate nonsense.

Avoid using one "trick" word in an otherwise correct response.

Keep the alternatives grammatically consistent with the stem.

Make all of the alternatives plausible.

Write the alternatives with similar grammatical construction, length, and degree of precision.

Restate laws, principles, and generalizations in words other than those used in actual instruction.

Write items so pupils will do the maximum amount of critical thinking, and minimum amount of recall or guessing.

Adapt the sample plan for a booklet by omitting the characters and skipping the dialogue.

Use the Content Outline to organize and write the booklet.

Write one right-answer page for every teaching point in the Content Outline.

Define each term and concept the first time they are used.

Direct a pupil who gives incorrect answers to a page that reteaches and sends him on to a new question.

Prepare your own auxiliary remedial material by taping the reteaching of the concept.

Recommend as much auxiliary material as you can in other media for reteaching.

Route a pupil who learns best in another modality away from the booklets into records, tapes, overhead visuals, films, filmstrips, manipulatory materials, etc.

Check your booklet for these things: no proofreading errors; all objectives and content are covered; the page numbers direct learners to the correct pages.

Plan the bubbles (numbered circles) on a Bubble Diagram so they represent all booklet pages, with the exception of one warning page.

Use a Bubble Diagram as a visual representation of the page organization of an intrinsic scrambled programmed book.

Plan a Bubble Diagram for scrambling the pages, or use the sample given, when the material for your booklet is written.

Arrange the booklet pages numerically. The scrambling will come automatically, due to the paging.

Keep a simple progress chart for each pupil working on programmed booklets.

List name, booklet, Pre-Test and Post-Test scores, as well as
booklets completed or skipped.

Write programmed booklets in workshop groups for your district,
or share and trade booklets with other teachers.

Sample Plan for
an Intrinsic Scrambled
Booklet

Chapter Three

This chapter contains material for you to use to make a sample programmed booklet in the scrambled style. Each page is separated by asterisks.

Freddy and the Subject   *Page 1*

Figure 3-1

Freddy: Well, here I am. I'm Freddy, Mr. . . .

Professor B.:   Professor Bumble is my name.

Freddy: Professor Bumble, what kind of a book is this? All I know is that it's about me.

Professor B.:   You'll have to find out for yourself. Choose the first answer by trying to guess. Do whatever one answer below tells you to do.

(a) Storybook. (Turn to Page 3.)
(b) Textbook. (Turn to Page 6.)
(c) Guessing game book. (Turn to Page 9.)
(d) All three of the above kinds. (Turn to Page 4.)

*   *   *   *   *   *   *   *

Page 2

Professor B.:   One thing I can tell you, Freddy, is that this book is not like others that you've read. You can't find *anything* by turning the pages. You must answer the questions and follow the directions in your answer or you'll get LOST! Please turn back to Page 1 and answer the question.

*   *   *   *   *   *   *   *

Page 3

YOUR ANSWER: Storybook.

Professor B.:   Don't be disappointed because this isn't a storybook, Freddy. Your answer was good because there *is* some story in it, and you're the main character. Turn to Page 5.

*   *   *   *   *   *   *   *

Page 4

YOUR ANSWER: All three of the above kinds.

Professor B.:　Correct! You're pretty sharp, Freddy — that means smart and wide-awake. Turn to Page 5.

*　*　*　*　*　*　*　*

Page 5

Professor B.:　This book may seem like a storybook or a textbook or a guessing game, but it's all three rolled into one. You're going to learn about an important part of a sentence called a *subject*. Since you're the main character, the story is really about you. You'll be asked to guess only once. You'll do much more than just guess on your answers. You might even be sure. Sometimes you can ask me questions too.

Freddy:　What's a subject? At first I thought it was a dragon or something, from the title of the book. Now I'm not so sure.

Professor B.:　Well, I admit it would have made it a more exciting book if the subject *were* a dragon, but you might still have to struggle with it a little bit, so this could be an adventure. Ready to meet it? Turn to Page 7.

*　*　*　*　*　*　*　*

Page 6

YOUR ANSWER: Textbook.

Professor B.:　You gave a good answer and it's almost correct. Don't give a sigh of relief because this isn't really a textbook. It's that — and much more. It has characters, it's like a game, and it's going to help you learn things on your own. Turn to Page 5.

*　*　*　*　*　*　*　*

Page 7

Freddy: I'm ready.
Professor B.:   I'm not.
Freddy: What's the matter?
Professor B.:   I lost my answers. I've got the question. Golly! Where did I put them? They were right here on this pile of old papers. Ah! Here they are! Why do you think you *need* to know what a subject in a sentence is at all? Choose an answer.

(a) Professor Bumble says so. (Turn to Page 8.)
(b) My mother will get mad if I don't. (Turn to Page 15.)
(c) I use subjects every time I write a sentence. (Turn to Page 11.)
(d) I'll need them some day for my future. (Turn to Page 16.)

*   *   *   *   *   *   *   *

Page 8

YOUR ANSWER: Professor Bumble says so.

Professor B.:   Ha! I really fooled you. I'd like to have you respect my wishes, but you'll never learn much from a reason like *that*. Turn to Page 7 and try Answer (c).

*   *   *   *   *   *   *   *

Page 9

YOUR ANSWER: Guessing game book.

Professor B.:   I don't blame you for choosing this answer, considering the way we're starting. You did a good job on answering your first question. This, however, is not a guessing game. In fact, I hope that you will really think before you decide on an answer. You're going to learn something you'll need. Turn to Page 5.

*   *   *   *   *   *   *   *

Page 10

YOUR ANSWER: The sad boy cried all the way home.

Professor B.:   Right! I told you that you could do it! You've really been an expert on English sentences since you've been a little boy — er — flea. You've been using them so long that you can't miss. You'll spot nonsense anytime. So, you see that good, sensible words aren't enough. They have to follow a special order that we're used to. The subject was "The sad boy."

Freddy: When do I get the tools?

Professor B.:   What tools?

Freddy: You promised me some before. You said we were going to build something.

Professor B.:   I sure did. With a memory like that, you should do very well. The first tool is coming right up. Turn to Page 17.

Page 17.

      *   *   ·*   *   *   *   *   *

Page 11

YOUR ANSWER: I use subjects every time I write a sentence.

Professor B.:   Right! Atta boy! You're really on the ball. That means you're sharp! Turn to Page 12.

Turn to Page 12.

      *   *   *   *   *   *   *   *

Page 12

Professor B.:   Sit still. You wiggle too much. Oh well, the *real* reason for learning subjects is that you need them all of the time. They're just like any other tool. We use them to build something.

Freddy: What?

Professor B.:   Sentences, and since you talk in sentences part of the time, and write in sentences all of the time, we don't have a second to waste! I'll get the next question. I didn't lose *this* one. I kept it in my pocket. Why are you wiggling around?

Freddy: What are my four choices?

Professor B.:   I was just asking you a question about yourself. You certainly do wiggle a lot. Turn to Page 13.

*   *   *   *   *   *   *   *

Page 13

Freddy: I can't help it.

Professor B.:   Where was I?

Freddy: You were in your pocket.

Professor B.:   Why?

Freddy: You were looking for the next question.

Professor B.:   Thanks, Freddy. We're really going to get along well, even though you do wiggle. I'm not going to tell you what a subject is yet. We're going to use some for a while so you can get to know them.

Freddy: O.K.

Professor B.:   All right — here are three groups of words. One of them is a sentence, and the other two groups make no sense at all, although you know each word. Select the real sentence.

Freddy: I didn't learn how yet.

Professor B.:   You can do it. Turn to Page 14 and try it.

*   *   *   *   *   *   *   *

Page 14

Freddy: I never heard of having a test before the lesson.

Professor B.:   Well, if you get stuck, I'll help you. How about that?

Freddy: That's fair.

Professor B.:   I've got the question and answers. Here they are! Select the one answer that makes sense.

(a) The boy sad cried the home all way. (Turn to Page 20.)
(b) Boy the sad cried the way all home. (Turn to Page 18.)
(c) The sad boy cried all the way home. (Turn to Page 10.)

*   *   *   *   *   *   *   *

Page 15

YOUR ANSWER: My mother will get mad if I don't.

Professor B.:   No, she won't! To her they're just the first tool in a big tool kit for building sentences. She's mighty nice, so give her a chance. Turn to Page 7 and choose Answer (c).

*   *   *   *   *   *   *   *

Page 16

YOUR ANSWER: I'll need them some day for my future.

Professor B.:   Well, that's a fine answer! But it isn't quite correct, because although you'll need subjects for your future too, what about *right now* when you need them? Let the future take care of itself. Turn to Page 7 and try Answer (c).

*   *   *   *   *   *   *   *

Page 17

Professor B.:   The sentence we're going to work with is: *The cat drinks milk.* Now, choose the sentence with the entire first part missing.
(a) The ____drinks milk. (Turn to Page 19.)
(b) ___ ___drinks milk. (Turn to Page 23.)
(c) The __ ____ milk. (Turn to Page 22.)

*   *   *   *   *   *   *   *

Page 18

YOUR ANSWER: Boy the sad cried the way all home.
Professor B.:   Come on now. You're just trying to fool me. You know that Sentence (b) doesn't make sense. Stick to the pages with the answers you really choose. Turn back to Page 14 and select Answer (c). You knew it.

*   *   *   *   *   *   *   *

Page 19

YOUR ANSWER: The____drinks milk.
Professor B.:   No. Well, you almost got it, Freddy, but since "The" is in the sentence, the *entire* first part isn't missing. Turn to Page 21.

*   *   *   *   *   *   *   *

Page 20

YOUR ANSWER: The boy sad cried the home all way.
Professor B.:   No. I know you're just peeking, Freddy. You're too smart to say that that sentence makes sense. Turn to Page 14 and select Answer (c).

*   *   *   *   *   *   *   *

Page 21

Professor B.: The *entire* first part of the sentence is missing. In this answer, it tells *who* drinks milk. What part is missing? Look back again at Page 17.

Freddy: "The cat."

Professor B.: Correct. By the way, if I wanted to tell someone about my teaching you, I'd have to say, "The little flea I work with every day is coming along very well with sentences." Can you think of something easier for me to call you than "The little flea I work with every day"?

Freddy: Freddy?

Professor B.: Very good! For the same reason, we give the name *subject* to the first part of a simple sentence. It's shorter and easier to use than saying, "The first part of a simple sentence."

Freddy: It sure is.

Professor B.: Turn to Page 24.

* * * * * * * *

Page 22

YOUR ANSWER: The __ ___ milk.

Professor B.: No. You chose the middle part, not the first part. Let's get up and stretch. You may need a little break. Ah!...That's better! Now, turn back to Page 17, and look at Answer (b). Take a good look at what I mean by the first part of a sentence. "The cat" was left out. O.K.? Turn to Page 21.

* * * * * * * *

Page 23

YOUR ANSWER: __ ___ drinks milk.

Professor B.: Right! Good work, Freddy! Turn to Page 21.

* * * * * * * *

Page 24

Professor B.: Do you think that you could select a sentence that has a missing subject?

Freddy: I don't know.

Professor B.: Here you are. Choose one.

(a) ___ ___ eats meat. (Turn to Page 28.)
(b) The ___ ___ meat. (Turn to Page 26.)
(c) The dog eats___ . (Turn to Page 27.)

*   *   *   *   *   *   *   *

Page 25

YOUR ANSWER: The cow___ ___ . OR The cow eats ___ .

Professor B.: No. Sorry. You chose the last part of the sentence for the subject, and I'm sure you'll remember that the subject is — where?

Freddy: At the start?

Professor B.: Good! You do know it. "The cow" is the subject, and it tells who eats grass. Where is a subject in a simple sentence?

Freddy: It starts it.

Professor B.: You've got it. What does the subject tell us about the sentence?

Freddy: I think it tells who does something.

Professor B.: Yes. So when I say this, tell me the subject. "I will see you tomorrow."

Freddy: I?

Professor B.: I'm proud of you, Freddy. Turn to Page 31.

*   *   *   *   *   *   *   *

Page 26

YOUR ANSWER: The ___ ___ meat.

Professor B.: Sorry. You chose a missing middle, Freddy. What were you asked to choose?

Freddy: A missing subject.

Professor B.:   Is the subject of a simple sentence in the middle?

Freddy: No. I forgot. Where is it?

Professor B.:   The subject is in the beginning of the sentence. In this sentence, the subject is "The dog," and it tells who eats meat. Let's have a little practice. Select the sentence with the missing subject. You can do it. Turn to Page 29.

*   *   *   *   *   *   *   *

Page 27

YOUR ANSWER: The dog eats____ .

Professor B.:   No. The sentence you chose had a missing end, my boy. You were asked to choose a missing subject. Where would you find the subject?

Freddy: I'm not sure.

Professor B.:   The subject is in the beginning of the sentence. In this sentence, the subject is "The dog," and it tells *who* eats meat. Let's have some practice with another sentence. Select the sentence with the missing subject. You can do it now. Turn to Page 29.

*   *   *   *   *   *   *   *

Page 28

YOUR ANSWER: ____ ____eats meat.

Professor B.:   Correct! You're great, Freddy! We can go right ahead as long as you're so good. The subject was "The dog," and it told *who* eats the meat.

Freddy: I know what a subject is now.

Professor B.:   Good. Where is it in a simple sentence?

Freddy: At the beginning.

Professor B.:   What does the subject do in the sentence?

Freddy: It tells *who* does whatever they do.

Professor B.:   Yes. It tells *who* or *what* the sentence is about. See you tomorrow.

Freddy: See ya.

*   *   *   *   *   *   *   *

Page 29

Professor B.:   (a)___ ____eats grass. (Turn to Page 30.)
(b) The cow___ ____ . (Turn to Page 25.)
(c) The cow eats ___ . (Turn to Page 25.)

*   *   *   *   *   *   *   *

Page 30

YOUR ANSWER:___ ____eats grass.

Professor B.:   You made it! You know that a subject comes where in a simple sentence?

Freddy: At the start?

Professor B.:   Right. What does it tell us?

Freddy: Who does something?

Professor B.:   Very good. Turn to Page 31.

*   *   *   *   *   *   *   *

Page 31

Professor B.:   I know that you know what a subject is, Freddy. This should be easy for you. You'll find a sentence repeated three times below. In each sentence, something different is underlined. I would like you to choose the sentence that has underlining under the subject.

Freddy: O.K.

(a) The horse eats <u>hay</u>. (Turn to Page 33.)
(b) <u>The horse</u> eats hay. (Turn to Page 32.)
(c) The horse <u>eats</u> hay. (Turn to Page 33.)

*   *   *   *   *   *   *   *

Page 32

YOUR ANSWER: <u>The horse</u> eats hay.

Professor B.: Fine work! See you tomorrow.

Freddy: See ya.

* * * * * * * *

Page 33

YOUR ANSWER: The horse eats <u>hay</u>. OR The horse <u>eats</u> hay.

Professor B.: Sorry. No. We still have a little work to do on subjects, Freddy. Tomorrow we're going to do something new. Thanks for trying so hard. See you next time.

Freddy: See ya.

Professor B.: Before you go, turn to Page 34.

* * * * * * * *

Page 34

Professor B.: Please bring this page to show your teacher in your regular class, Freddy. She may have a record for you to hear, or something else interesting to do. I'll see you soon.

Freddy: See ya.

Figure 3-2

Suggestions: Specially prepared record for series.

Color filmstrip — *Using Good English* series "Building Good Sentences." Filmstrip No. 130-1, 40 frames. Consultant — Harold G. Shane, University Professor of Education, Indiana University Society for Visual Education, Inc.

Filmstrip — *Pilot to Good English* series — 109300 "Learning About Simple Sentences," L.C.FiA 52-1633, about 50 frames. McGraw-Hill.

*   *   *   *   *   *   *   *

Ideas for Those
with an Aptitude
in Social Studies

Chapter Four

Try to emphasize *people* in your teaching of social studies. We underplay that at times and tend to concentrate on human institutions. It will fascinate your students to study human institutions as something designed by people for people. Study the beginnings of human institutions, and the cases where they went wrong and no longer served the people, but began to rule them or harm them. This may be a very new viewpoint for your students.

From your bright children you should expect a great deal of reading of history and books about other cultures, as well as extensive practice in map, globe, and research skills. A wide knowledge of history is needed as a background for understanding the present. Facts, the ability to discover facts, and research skills, are the basis for good judgment in understanding social structures and problems. Most important of all, teach youngsters to look for the organization of these facts in a pattern (sometimes a repeating one) — the vast periods of history, the influences of industrialization on politics, the many causes for events, etc.

You will find some overlapping between this chapter and a few others. First of all, because social studies activities go so well with writing and art, you will also find some activities related to social studies in Chapter One, "Challenging the Verbally Bright," and Chapter Five, "Ideas for Those Who Are Talented in the Arts." Second, because social studies are taught so well by games, you will find social studies material in Chapter Nine, "Using Games to Stimulate Bright Children."

In this chapter, you'll find some suggestions for identifying children who have an aptitude in social studies. There are ideas for adding interest to economics. You'll read how to play "Community Treasure Hunt," a "Mapdown" game, "Blind Man's Travels," "Where Am I?", and "Grab-a-State." You will learn how to use postcards from imaginary travels, music, buzz sessions, and World Pen Pals as social studies activities. Ideas are also given for a special club for those with an aptitude and interest in social studies.

Suggestions for Identifying Them

Rather than be frustrated at the difficulty of identifying those with special aptitudes in social studies, be glad about the unlimited opportunities you have to intrigue all students. The variety of possible aptitudes and interests in the social studies are as vast as the many aspects of the study of man and his institutions. You are bound to find something that interests each child, whether it is the study of American Indians, the reading of road maps, or interest in elections.

There are some general guidelines for spotting those with unusual talent, but they will also apply to talent in many other school subjects. This kind of student usually does well in achievement tests. He loves to read about faraway people and places. He is alert, gives answers in depth when asked questions, supplies details, and qualifies his answers. This type of child can guess what the teacher might want him to say. His facts are likely to be correct, and he shows facility with most study skills. He uses all kinds of references well, and he enjoys digging information out of them. Encyclopedias, almanacs, maps, globes, and card catalogues intrigue him. He has a time perspective, and shows interest in the past as well as the future. A student like this looks for relationships and causes. He likes to ask, "What would have happened if this had been different?"

"Community Treasure Hunt"

This would be a good after-school voluntary activity, or it could be conducted as a field trip during school hours for upper elementary students. Plan it for a clear, mild day in spring or fall. Get written parental permission.

The "treasure" could be anything at all that you choose to give. One suggestion is a small pencil sharpener shaped like a world globe for each member of the winning team.

Divide the players into five or six teams. Each team would start out with a copy of a simple neighborhood map that gives all of the street names, important buildings, and landmarks in the neighborhood near the school. With the map, each team would receive its first clue, which would be in rhyme. The clue would lead the children to the first stop, where they receive their clue to the next stop, and so on. All places should be ones that students would be familiar with, and close enough to be available to children by bicycling or walking.

Before the Treasure Hunt, arrange the cooperation of each place where the children will receive clues. Avoid bothering business establishments. You can choose obvious places where you could station selected helpers to give out the clues.

The clues do not have to be funny. They need to be clearly written in ink in manuscript writing, and they should give enough information to lead students on to the next clue. An example of a clue could be:

Analyze these words well.
Washington never took alarm and *dodged* his responsibilities. Maybe this will ring a bell. On a job like this he wouldn't freeze.

Hopefully, this clue would lead students to the familiar Washington and Dodge Streets, where they will find a classmate giving out clues in front of a fire station. In case they don't figure out the clue, the map they have may suggest what it means when they read through its street names and labeled locations.

Try not to send students anywhere near heavy traffic areas. If there's a regularly scheduled bookmobile, a museum, or a library nearby that you'd like the children to become more familiar with, direct them to it with one of the clues.

Aside from the obvious fun, this game will give students some practice in using a street map, and it will help them become more familiar with their community.

"Mapdown" Game

Although competitive in nature, try to conduct this game in a spirit of teamwork and fun. It combines some features of a spelldown with practice in locating places on a map. It would be most useful as a review at the conclusion of intensive map study of North America. Begin with simple places that will be easy to find, and progress to the more difficult ones. Try to use locations that are important in human geography in some way. They could be well-known for political, industrial, or recreational reasons. Don't use the names of obscure mountains or streams that nobody knows (or cares to know).

Divide the class into two even teams. You should conduct the game and function as timekeeper. Allow plenty of time for the game. Give the first player a pointer and a piece of chalk. Keep the map out of sight until the player spells the name of the place by writing it on the board. Call out a "place name" for the student to spell on the board. Once he puts down the chalk, he may not change the spelling. Capitalization is necessary to be correct. After the name is written, the player pulls down the map and uses the pointer to point to the place on the map. He must do this within a half-minute time limit. If the pointer is fairly near the correct place, count the player as correct. If he points to an incorrect place on the map, or if he cannot find the place within the time limit, the player must sit down and be out of the game. Check the spelling of each name as soon as the place has been correctly located. If the spelling is correct and the place is located, give the player's team one point. If not, write the name correctly so that everyone can see it and show the correct location. Then go on to the next name. The next player would come from the other team.

The game ends when only one student is left standing or when the time is up. The winning team is the one with the most players or the most points when the game ends. If one team has more players and the other has the most points at the end of the game, consider it a tie.

A few suggested places that students should know in North America are given here:

Washington, D.C.	the Mississippi River
Texas	Canada
Mexico	Alaska
Hawaii	California
Lake Ontario	Lake Erie
Lake Superior	Lake Michigan
Lake Huron	the Rocky Mountains
Yellowstone National Park	Hudson Bay
the St. Lawrence River	Cape Cod

"Blind Man's Travels"

This challenging game can only be played after a study of North America. It will provide some excellent review. It could be played by individuals or by teams.

Students take turns at a map of North America, with a blindfold on. Place a pointer in the student's hand and ask him to point somewhere on the map. Wherever he points is his topic. He must give a correct product, industry, recreational feature, or topographical fact about the particular city, state, or region. Be very generous in accepting all answers, as this is a difficult game to play. After an answer is accepted, ask for suggestions from the class. This will broaden the scope of the answers and give you an opportunity to add something, if you wish. Students who cannot answer, or who give incorrect answers, are eliminated from the game until a winner is left. The game is over when only one student remains standing, or when you run out of time. If you play with teams, the team with the most players at the end of the game is the winner.

Make reference books available and have a few students with special aptitude act as librarians. Don't hesitate to have them check dubious information. If you don't do it too often, the checking and the adding of new information from references will enhance your review game. It will be helpful to you too, as no one knows as much as he needs to for this game.

"Where Am I?"

The following game can also be used after study of a particular area. Because those who live in a place learn more about it and tend to travel there more, it would probably be best to limit the game to your own part of the world.

Divide the class into two equal teams who will stand opposite each other. The first person in Team One begins with a question, and the first one in Team Two must answer. If he answers correctly, the next person in Team Two asks a question of the next one in line for Team One. The questions and answers will continue in an alternate way, to give everyone on each side a turn. If a player answers incorrectly, or cannot answer, he sits down and is out of the game. The next person in his team tries to answer the same question, and this continues until a correct answer is given. The game is over when only one player is left, or when the time is up. The winning team is the one with the most players at the end of the game.

The game is played in this way. The questioner might say: "I am on top of the highest mountain in the United States. Where am I?" The questions can refer to any place in North America that students might be expected to know. If you think that a place is too obscure, ask the questioner to go on to the next person with a better question.

This game, needless to say, will also be challenging for the teacher, who must decide if the answers are correct. Do not be embarrassed to use your student librarians for reference at all times. In case you and your helpers cannot find the correct answer, or if you disagree with the questioner about one of his statements, allow the player to remain in the game and go on to the next player in his team for a new question. Save all unanswered questions and questionable statements for a very rewarding session later, after you find out the answers.

Postcards from Imaginary Travels

This activity will be valuable for all of your students. Those with special aptitude will probably put more effort into it.

Each student is to choose a place where he would like to imagine he has gone for a vacation. His task is to use all available reference books (and his imagination) to draw and color a postcard picture on one side of his paper. On the other side, he is to write a postcard to the class, in which he tells at least three interesting facts about the place he is "visiting."

Encourage free movement to encyclopedias and to the library for this activity. Allow enough time for interested students to really dig into their topic. Expect to receive many postcards from the moon, Mars, and Venus. It will be fun to discuss how your travelers survived at vacation spots that have inhospitable atmospheres.

How to Play "Grab-a-State"

Explain to the class that this activity starts out like a grab bag game, and that it ends up with written committee reports organized into a class notebook.

Prepare a grab bag by filling a large paper bag with puzzle pieces of the 50 states. Give each child a chance to pull one state from the bag.

Have a large wall map of the United States displayed for reference. The children will need this when they organize into committees to study regions of the United States. Help them, if necessary, in decisions on border states. Allow some time for them to get together into committees and decide who belongs where. This will be rather hectic, but very enjoyable and worthwhile.

Choose, or have each committee select, a chairman for each group. The individuals on each committee are responsible for a written report on important features of their states. Specify what information each report should contain. The chairman organizes them to also prepare a short group report on the general climate, topography, industries, and distinguishing features of each region.

You may have Alaska and Hawaii work together, if these two states are pulled from the grab bag. If only one is pulled, have this state work with the Pacific Region.

When each region report is ready, help the chairmen organize the reports into a notebook. You may wish to have each individual state report follow a color map of the state in the notebook. The region sections can be identified by region maps.

As always, some interested (and talented?) students will prepare their individual state reports, help with the group region report, and still have time left. Encourage these children to reach in the grab bag for another state (if any are left), and investigate it in any way they wish — draw a map of it, go to the library to see a filmstrip about it, draw a picture showing an important place in the state, etc. Don't require another report, as the children will probably have had enough of reports by that time. If you have a system of awarding extra credits, this will be an opportunity to give rewards for extra effort. In case these students do not wish to "grab" another state from the bag, give them the choice of helping someone else finish up a report, or a free reading or game time.

Adding Interest to Economics

If you have ever listened to a group of business people talking about how they earn their livings, you know how very exciting the subject can be. To keep the excitement of real life, try the simulation games that are used so well in the social studies. Teach inductively through a "discovery" method based on real-life situations.

"The Game of Market,"[1] a simulation designed to assist upper elementary children in understanding the principles of supply and demand, will actively involve its players. See Chapter Nine for a brief description of the original version, and a discussion on simulation games. It will be well worth the entire week of social studies time it takes to play this game twice, as a second play is recommended. Have players reverse as many roles as

---

[1] "The Game of Market," Elementary Economics III — Unit Two, Industrial Relations Center, the University of Chicago, Copyright, 1967. Developed from the original version of Abt Associates, Inc., 55 Wheeler Street, Cambridge, Massachusetts 02138.

possible on the second playing. Each team has two players. There will be two winning teams, one from the Retailers and one from the Consumers.

A Retailer team wins by selling the Food Cards it has purchased from the Wholesaler at prices higher than its costs. The costs are the wholesale prices of the goods plus the $1 rental price of the Retailer team's location. Retailer team members accomplish this by selling more Food Cards, at competitive prices which are above costs.

The winning Consumer team wins by purchasing more Food Cards than the other teams in an effort to fill its 30-space Shopping Board. At the same time, the team members complete the requirements for six dinner meals. They receive points for satisfying these requirements, and points are also given for money not spent at the end of the game.

Plan on the post-game discussion, which is just as important as the game.

Life on Paradise Island[2] is a fine paperback that introduces some elementary principles of economics in a unique way that children can relate to their own lives. This book tells a story that focuses on the evolving economic life of the fictional Jubilant Tribe on imaginary Paradise Island.

The story begins with the islanders' very simple life as each family took care of its own needs, and goes on as their society evolved and became more advanced. First, barter was discovered as families began to trade. This led to specialization, and the islanders came to depend on each other for the goods and services they needed. As the population increased and land grew scarce, the concept of private property developed. Labor, or helping hands, brought about wages. The islanders needed a place to store their goods, or wealth, so a bank was established. Money was invented, and laws, taxation, and public services were begun for the common good. This led to a representative government. Then the islanders began bartering goods and started foreign trade with their neighbors on Plentiful Island. Businesses, unions, and insurance resulted. Then war broke out between the people of the two

---

[2] W. Harmon Wilson and Roman F. Warmke, *Life on Paradise Island* (Glenview, Illinois: Scott, Foresman and Company, 1970).

islands, causing inflation and full employment. The story tells how the economy had to adjust to peace when the war ended, and how the islanders lived through deflation and unemployment.

The cartoon-like drawings and readable writing style keep the reader's interest. Each chapter ends with a questions section that helps you evaluate your students' understanding of the ideas presented. The three-page Appendix will help students with special aptitude to go on to think of their own economy and that of other modern societies in terms of the basic concepts learned.

Using Music

One of the most effective ways to stimulate interest in other people and other lands is to play recordings of their music. Use records and tapes to enrich your regularly scheduled social studies lessons. Music will also be a fine way to entice your students with special aptitudes into doing independent study of people in other lands. Provide provocative recordings that will interest youngsters in many different cultures. This will help them choose what they would like to investigate on their own.

Some records that could interest students in new places are:

Harry Belafonte, "Calypso"[3]
Fikret Amirov, "Caucasian Dances"[4]
Leonard Pennario, "An American in Paris"[5]
Ronnie Gilbert, James Justice, The Spotlight Singers, "Spotlight on Africa"[6]

Learning from Buzz Sessions

Classroom buzz sessions are different from committee work

---

[3] Harry Belafonte, "Calypso," Radio Corporation of America, 33-1/3 R.P.M., LPM-1248.

[4] Fikret Amirov, Symphony Orchestra of Radio Leipzig, "Caucasian Dances," Urania Record Corp., 160 Passaic Ave., Kearny, N.J., 33-1/3 R.P.M., Mono, UR-7117.

[5] Leonard Pennario, "An American in Paris," Capitol Records, 33-1/3 R.P.M., T1678, Side 2.

[6] Ronnie Gilbert, James Justice, The Spotlight Singers, "Spotlight on Africa," Hy Zaret and Lou Singer, Motivation Records, "Spotlight Ballads to Light Up the World," 33-1/3 R.P.M., MRBX2.

in several ways. When children work in committees they usually use references and work together to prepare a written report of some kind. They are generally working on a particular topic, about which they are trying to find more information. For example, they may be studying "Pollution of American Cities." In buzz sessions, however, the children usually work together in a different way. They talk rather than read and write, and they work with opinions more than with facts. Their chairman tries to get a consensus about the topic. (This is a fine responsibility for students who have an aptitude in social studies.) If the chairman cannot achieve agreement, the group reports a majority and a minority opinion when it is time for the buzz session group to share its findings with the rest of the class. In a buzz session, the topic is usually a question rather than a specific fact that is to be investigated. For instance, a good buzz session question could be: "Should the use of automobiles by private citizens be restricted in American cities?"

Give some guidance to the chairmen of groups before the buzz sessions begin. You might suggest the following guidelines:

Keep your group members polite to each other.
Remind members to listen to each other and answer each other rather than give speeches.
Give equal turns to each member, and limit harangues.
Allow no shouting, sarcasm, or insults.
Try to keep students on the topic question.
Jot down *any* statements that show possible agreement.
Five minutes before the buzz sessions are over, use your notes to sum up any agreements the group has reached.
If opinion is split, report both majority and minority opinions in a way that has been approved by the group's members.

Any controversial question of general interest will be a good topic for buzz sessions. If you select a topic that will be answered in the same way by every student, you will end up with quick agreement and no discussion. How controversial you wish to get depends a great deal upon the age of your students and how brave you are. Buzz sessions of some kind could be profitably started with students as young as those in the fourth grade. Try to choose a subject about which children have some knowledge, and find one in which they have some personal involvement. If students know nothing about the subject, they'll have nothing worthwhile to say. If the topic is too far removed from their own lives, most of the students will be too bored with it to get a good discussion going.

Some possible buzz session topics for upper-grade students that will cause a stir are:

"Should the schools be in session all year, with staggered vacations?"

"Should young women be drafted for some kind of government service?"

"Should football and boxing be ended as school and professional sports for safety reasons?"

"Should every citizen who wants one be guaranteed a job?"

"Should schools televise their lessons for home study?"

In case you wonder what your class would get out of the buzz sessions that would justify the time spent on them, there are obvious as well as subtle benefits. It is good for students to learn how to get together in a group and talk about a question in an organized way. Too often people become adults without any practice in discussion. They become the shouters. In their inability to discuss differences in a rational way, they become frustrated and abusive. They scream, repeat an opinion over and over again, and refuse to listen to anyone else's viewpoint. If students get practice in buzz sessions, they will be led to listen to others, they will try to help others to reach agreement, and they will become willing occasionally to change an opinion. Your able students who serve as chairmen will benefit from the practice in leadership skills, the organizing of opinions they must do, and the responsibility they must take. If discussion techniques are practiced often, students will learn how to talk to others (and more important, how to *listen* to them).

World Pen Pals[7]

A 19-year-old girl from Lebanon, Oregon wrote the following after returning from visiting her pen pal in Greece:

---

[7]Mrs. Virginia Stevens, Executive Secretary, World Pen Pals, University of Minnesota, Minneapolis, Minnesota 55414.

> "I owe the happiness of this visit to you people.
> You may have sent only a slip of paper with a name on
> it four years ago, but from this has grown a friendship
> that will last as long as the mail goes through!"

Encourage your pupils to have the satisfying experience of
writing to a boy or girl abroad. World Pen Pals receives many
thousands of names from abroad, a great number of them from
Africa and Asia. These young people are eager for friends from the
United States, ages 12 to 19. However, World Pen Pals often runs
short of children from abroad under age 14.

Teachers with students who wish to have a foreign pen pal
may send away to the organization for them. Do not send lists of
names nor ask your students to write individually. All that is
required is the number of boys and their ages, number of girls and
ages, and a 35-cent group service charge for each student. Names
and material will be sent in one packet to the teacher or group
leader. Individual young people from the United States who wish
to correspond with a pen pal abroad may contact the World Pen
Pals organization, which will send them an application to fill out.
If students write individually, the service fee is 50 cents.

Each applicant will receive the name of a foreign youth who
has requested a U.S. pen pal. The foreign name is selected by
World Pen Pals from individual letters and lists it receives from
well-established correspondence organizations abroad: schools, the
U.S. Information Agency, Peace Corps volunteers, Voice of
America, Radio Free Europe, articles in youth publications, and
similar sources. There is no service charge to the foreign pen pal.

Pen friend letters from overseas are usually written in English
(which is widely understood throughout the world). Girls who
request boy correspondents may be given a girl instead, since few
boys here or abroad request female pen friends.

"The Silver Lining" Pen Pal newspaper and a suggestion sheet
for good letter writing are included with each pen pal.

If you have gifted older students able to correspond in
French, German, Spanish, or Portuguese, request pen pals abroad
who wish to correspond in these particular languages, as the
Executive Secretary says that they often have letters written in
these four languages.

The main purpose of this international non-political, non-profit, inter-racial, and non-creedal organization is to bring to young people of the world a better understanding of each other through friendly letter writing. World Pen Pals prefers that students not be required to have a pen pal as a class assignment or for extra credit. A lasting, friendly correspondence usually does not develop unless it is voluntary.

The organization does not link U.S. classes with classes abroad. Their service is for individuals only. They ask to choose the country for you, as it may be impossible to give students any country they wish, due to age and language barriers.

Some helpful suggestions given by the organization are:

A.   When you receive your foreign pen pal, *you* write to him first, as soon as possible, using an Air Letter (sold at post offices). This is a quick and inexpensive way to establish contact and to let him know the basic facts of who you are and why you are writing.

B.   For future letters use lightweight stationery and envelopes or Air Letters.

C.   *Print* or *type* your name and complete return address both on the inside of the letter and on the envelope.

D.   *Be certain* that your name, street address, city, state, zip code, and USA are readable. Make figures carefully and do not abbreviate.

E.   *Before you write* be sure to locate your pen pal's home on the map and learn about the geography and history of his country. *Imagine you are talking with your new friend.*

F.   Write about your personal life. Tell who you are, describe your family, where you live, what you like to do, or tell about a typical day.

G.   Tell of hobbies, sports, pets, holidays, school, special customs, books, clubs, church — anything unique and interesting to a stranger to the USA; games, recipes, art, or music could be included.

H.   Tell of your town, state, country, and its history.

I.   Exchange snapshots, postcards, maps, books, magazines, records, tapes, and scrapbooks. Expensive gifts are not recommended.

J.   Ask questions of your pen pals about their lives, customs, country, schools, and hopes for peace. Give personal news and current events, stressing the positive. Exchange ideas.

K.   Take an interest in learning words and phrases in your pen pal's native language.

L.   Avoid fancy or unusual writing, slang, or bragging. Be courteous, sincere, and friendly. People abroad judge you, your school, and your country by your letters.

A Sample Lesson

The following lesson about Japan was created by Janet Yearout, a teacher in a special program for the gifted for children in grades one through three:[8]

I. *Overall Purpose:* To deepen children's understanding of people in other lands.

II. *Today's Objective:* To introduce children to the culture of Japan.

III. *General Procedure:* Discussion and art activity.

IV. *Background:* As each of the preceding lessons has dealt with life in a different country, the children should be able to make meaningful comparisons and contrasts about life in different cultures.

V. *Materials:* Shari Lewis and Lillian Oppenheimer, *Folding Paper Masks* (New York: E.P. Dutton and Company, 1965).

Art Materials: Construction paper, crayons, and Magic Markers.

Filmstrip: "Japanese Children."[9]

Record: "A Child's Introduction to Life in Japan and Burma."[10]

---

[8] Janet Yearout, M.A., Enhanced Learning Program for Gifted, Pinellas County Schools, Clearwater, Florida.

[9] "Japanese Children," Children of Many Lands, 16 FA B+W, 96FRS, Encyclopaedia Britannica Educational Corp. Film Library, 1822 Pickwick Ave., Glenview, Illinois 60025.

[10] Christobel Weerasing, "A Child's Introduction to Life in Japan and Burma," Wonderland Records, 235 W. 46th St., New York, N.Y., sponsored by World Federation of United Nations Association, CM1494.

VI. *Activities: Introductory Activity* — Play Japanese music. What do you think about when you hear this music? Guess what country we will be discussing today.

Activity — View the filmstrip. Discuss differences and similarities in Japanese and American life. Listen to Japanese folk tale, "Shining Beauty," on the record. How did the bamboo cutter feel when he found Shining Beauty? Why did Shining Beauty ask for impossible gifts? How do you suppose this story came to be written? Could you think of a different name for it? A different ending? How is it different from American folk tales?

Culminating Activity — Children will make original masks using the techniques of origami.

VII. *Follow-Up and Assignment:* Think during the week of how your life would be different if you were a Japanese child.

VIII. *Evaluation:* Were the children able to compare and contrast American and Japanese culture? Were the children good at listening? Were they thoughtful when discussing? Did the students enjoy the paper-folding activity? Was their work original?

The Excited Explorers and the Hysterical Historians — a Club

The child who has a special interest or aptitude in any of the social studies can benefit from a special club that provides challenging activities and games. This club, like the one you could have for those with extra talent or interest in the arts, could be enjoyed by many of your students because of the wide range of interests it could cover.

This type of child needs to expand his horizons. Encourage his special interest in time and space by providing a variety of people and places to find out about.

Have an Idea Box for independent study ideas. You may start excited research with something as small as a picture postcard from an exotic place, a recording of African tribal music, or a travel folder.

Provide extra training and practice in map, globe, and study skills. *Learning to Use a Map* is a fine booklet that is especially good for independent work.[11] It teaches everything a pupil needs to know about map reading, from finding directions on a map to

---

[11] Parmer L. Ewing, School of Education, New York University and Ronald O. Smith, Supervisor of Social Studies, Portland, Oregon, *Learning to Use a Map* (Chicago: A.J. Nystrom & Company, Third Edition, 1967).

telling time from maps. A child can work on his own with it by looking at the clear diagrams, reading the questions, and writing his answers on a piece of paper. Then he can check his work with the answers that are given upside-down on another page. He will learn not only a map vocabulary, but also all of the skills needed to use many kinds of maps.

Some of your club members will enjoy memorizing names of states or state capitals. (Which they choose to do would depend on their age.) Have a United States map on display at all times. Near it provide a stack of blank outline maps. Certain students will find it very enjoyable and challenging to try to fill in these facts from memory. They can keep trying until they achieve their goal. After you have checked their maps and made sure that they have memorized it all, you could post the students' names on a wall chart that says, "We Know Them All."[12] This particular activity should be an optional one.

A club activity requiring time and effort, but which would be fascinating to some of your students, is the writing of diaries. Make up a list of famous people or people who participated in historic events. Allow each interested member to select one person whose role he is to play as he writes his diary. He may decide to substitute another famous person or event to write about. Some possible diary "authors" could be:

> a soldier on duty with George Washington's army at Valley Forge.
> Genghis Khan as he invaded China
> a Roman gladiator after an exhibition
> a Tibetan lama in a Himalayan monastery
> John Wilkes Booth after Lincoln's assassination
> a spy during the Civil War
> a slave trader on board his ship, headed back to the United States with a load of slaves
> Daniel Boone as he explored Kentucky

Provide ample reference material. The more reading and researching a student has to do, the better his diary will be, and the more satisfaction he will take in it. Display the completed diaries in the school library on a special table, and allow other students to borrow and read diaries from the exhibit.

---

[12] Margaret Goldman, Middlefork School, Sunset Ridge School District #29, Northfield, Illinois.

Your members will enjoy playing any type of game. An interesting thinking game for older students is "The Propaganda Game."[13] Its goal is clear thinking, and it uses the method of identifying propaganda techniques. Players use Technique Cards with Prediction Dials, Example Dials, and a humorous Clear Thinking Chart. At the top of this chart we have the "Clear Thinker," which is the top attainment level. The bottom contains the "Ding-a-Ling Section." Awareness of propaganda methods is so important that the club members should teach this game to other class members in their spare time.

CHECKLIST

Try to emphasize *people* rather than their institutions.

Expect your bright students to read extensively about history and other cultures and to practice map, globe, and research skills.

Teach youngsters to look for facts, and for the organization of these facts in patterns.

Interest all of your students with the wide range provided by the social studies.

Try to identify students with aptitude in the social studies by these things:

They usually do much reading about faraway people and places.

They do well in achievement tests.

They are alert, questioning, and they answer questions in depth, with many details and qualifications.

They show interest in the past and the future, and they show facility with most study skills.

Give students practice in using street maps, and help them to become familiar with their community by having a "Community Treasure Hunt."

---

[13] Robert W. Allen and Lorne Green. "The Propaganda Game," based on the book *Thinking Straighter* by George Henry Moulds. AIM (Autotelic Instructional Materials) Publishers, New Haven, Conn., 1969.

Help pupils review map work with the "Mapdown" game, in which they spell the name and find a stated place on a map.

Use "Blind Man's Travels" to help students review geographical knowledge of North America by providing information about a given spot on a map.

Play "Where Am I?," the guessing game that reviews important places in North America.

Have students write and draw postcards from imaginary travels.

Have students play "Grab-a-State" by pulling state jigsaw puzzle pieces from a grab bag, and by writing individual state reports with maps. Use talented children as chairmen of groups that study and report on regions of the United States, and have them organize the available states into regions.

Keep the excitement of real life by teaching social studies with simulation games.

Make music one of your most frequently used tools for stimulating interest in other cultures.

Use buzz sessions often to teach and practice discussion techniques, using controversial topics.

Encourage some of your interested older students to correspond with overseas pen pals.

Use a special club to challenge children who show aptitude or interest in the social studies.

Ideas for Those
Who Are Talented
in the Arts

Chapter Five

Because the arts are human works of beauty and creativity, there are many different kinds — and most children enjoy participating in all of their rich variety. In the schools, there are usually opportunities for drawing and painting, writing, handicrafts, music, or creative dramatics.

This chapter will provide some help in identifying the talented child. It will tell ways to cultivate a capacity for aesthetic response and how to guide children in expressing feelings through the arts. There are sections on creating self-portraits by cutting and folding paper, figure drawing with models, and how to make a diorama. Suggestions are given for creating a pipe cleaner city, using collage, and making a research mural. A way to use a play as a core curriculum is described. Last, activities are suggested for a special club for those children who are talented and interested in the arts.

Identifying the Talented Child

Talent in the arts is probably more widespread and more

difficult to identify than any other kind. First, there are so many different kinds of artistic expression. Second, it is tremendously difficult, even for experts, to select the talented from the very many who show interest and enjoyment. The "fun" aspect of painting, making things, acting, and singing makes these activities almost as popular at school as gym and recess.

There are no tests that are really satisfactory for identifying talent in the fine arts. In painting or writing, the best test is a sample of the child's work judged by an expert. In dramatics, the best test is an audition for experts. A musical expert can make a judgment by listening to a child sing or play an instrument. He observes enjoyment, sensitivity to music, response to rhythms, and good memory for musical notes and phrases. It has been noted that people who are highly talented in the fine arts are usually above average intellectually. For the classroom teacher, if you observe a combination of outstandingly beautiful or original creations, as well as extreme perseverance and interest, you can assume some talent. Watch for reorganization of a subject in a child's artwork. This can be considered better than strictly realistic work, as the child is distilling and creating rather than copying.

Each pupil in your class should be given opportunities to express himself in as many of the arts as time allows. Here is your opportunity to build up each child's opinion of himself. You will almost surely find some artistic activity in which he can excel. A child who cannot read musical notes may have an unfailing rhythmic sense. Someone who cannot act before a group may be able to write a beautiful play for the others to act in. A pupil who can't write plays or stories may be able to create beautiful poems. A child who cannot sing or play an instrument may respond to music with creative dancing. Someone who is unable to draw and paint may have great patience and skill for paper construction. Search for the talented by giving children a variety of expression. Talent in the arts, like creativity, needs encouragement, opportunities, and practice. Identification is not your prime goal. If each child has many chances to try to draw, sing, write creatively, make things, dance, play an instrument, and act, you can relax about whether you have found and encouraged the talented. The very outstanding ones *may* show up, but each child's exposure to and enjoyment of the arts is more important.

Cultivating a Capacity for Aesthetic Response

The following lesson from *Art Learning Situations for Elementary Education* will be very stimulating for all fifth or sixth grade students who have studied texture, shapes, and unity in composition.[1]

The Objective

Cultivation of a capacity for aesthetic response.

The Situation . . . .

What next? "Complete" a painting that has been partially obscured.

Materials

Obtain two large reproductions of work by Gauguin and Kandinski or Miró that are "new" to the group. Cover them with white paper. From the white paper, cut two or three openings that expose small but significant areas of the composition. Provide each person with crayons and white drawing paper trimmed to correspond with the size of the reproduction.

Stimulation

Display the masked-off Gauguin (or other expressionistic painting that contains "simplified" subject matter). Ask some children to describe what they see in the exposed area. It is likely that many descriptions will pertain to *subject matter*; e.g., "There are plants and a woman against a white background." Gather several observations. Then, ask them how they would complete the picture. Again, several will probably respond in terms of subject matter proposals; a dog and a tree might add something to the scene. Upon receipt of the observations and proposals for completion, invite them to look at the *colors* present within the exposed subject matter. In what way and where could they be used again? Notice the *shapes*. What characteristics do they have (dark outlines in Gauguin), that would have to be repeated to insure *unity* in the *composition?* Focus more and more on the visual *elements* of the picture as a composition. Renew the discussion on the basis of this visually oriented approach.

---

[1] Warren Anderson, *Art Learning Situations for Elementary Education* (Belmont, California: Wadsworth Publishing Company, Inc., 1965), p. 95.

Procedure

Introduce a *non-objective* composition, appropriately masked off with a few vital areas exposed. The lack of subject matter may enable many of the children to focus upon the visible shapes, textures, and colors solely as shapes, textures, and colors. Suggest this possibility. Suspend any further discussion, however, of the possible ways in which the composition could be completed.

Distribute the art materials. Then ask the children to reproduce, as closely as possible, the two or three exposed shapes and colors of the non-objective painting. Using these as a nucleus, they should proceed with the remainder of the composition until much of the format is covered. Upon completion, unveil the masked-off masterpiece.

Indicate first of all that the intent is not that of matching the master (a remote possibility). Instead, study the different arrangements that evolved within the group as visual possibilities triggered by the initial stimulus . . . .Compare differences between their work and that of the mature painter. What did they do that seems to them to be more successful than his work, or, in many instances, less successful? . . .Try looking at both endeavors from different directions. Display some drawings, and respond to them aesthetically as "things in themselves."

Use the works of great artists to stimulate aesthetic appreciation. A series of books called *Art for Children* will be very useful to you in teaching about great artists in an interesting way. One of the books, *Henri Rousseau*,[2] reproduces the artist's most famous paintings, and describes the pictures, giving facts about the artist's life. Some of the pictures are described in the artists's own words, in excerpts from his letters. Color is used very effectively in the text part of this book to make it readable and exciting.

A child who shows talent in music will benefit from a variety of musical activities — singing, playing a simple instrument, listening to good records, expressing the rhythm in bodily movements, and studying the structure of music. "Hello, I'm Music!"[3] is a series of six sets of coordinated materials presenting

---

[2] Ernest Raboff, *Henri Rousseau, Art for Children*, A Gemini-Smith Book (Garden City, New York: Doubleday & Co., Inc., 1970).

[3] George Makas, Ed. D., Wm. Rainey Harper College, "Hello, I'm Music!", copyright MCMLXVIII, emc corporation, 180 East Sixth Street, St. Paul, Minnesota 55101.

information on the structure of music. It can be adapted and used for upper elementary through high school students. Each set contains a full-color filmstrip, an LP record, student study sheets, and a teacher's guide. Melody, rhythm, harmony, form, and tone color are explored. Information is presented by a cartoon character called "Music." This series can be used independently with a filmstrip previewer.

Expressing Feelings Through the Arts[4]

Purpose

To expose pupils to different art forms — music, poetry, paintings — and to illustrate that the connecting thread in all of them is expression of feeling. After pupils are aware of the fact that poetry, visual art (films included), and music all can express feelings of the artist, or establish a mood, the discussion (for older children — junior high) could lead into the different uses of space and time to create these moods/feelings.

— How e.e.cummings uses a page to create a visual pattern as well as a sound pattern.
— How color, paint strokes, different page placements, can influence feelings created by a painting.

Grade Level

Such a project could be carried out most successfully in the sixth to ninth grades. A child of this age group is becoming very concerned with his own body and his feelings. In discussing the feelings and moods as seen in the arts, children could then go into a project where they try to create a specific feeling by using one of the media. In doing so they have to explore what feelings are and how one projects them.

Materials

1. Various art plates/books of paintings by various artists, starting with the Romantic Era, going to impressionists, expressionists, and abstract expressionists. Portraits of people should be used as illustrations. Most examples should be in color. A few black-and-whites of some of the color prints could be used to illustrate what happens with the absence of color.

---

[4] Laura Joseph, B.S. Degree Art Ed., University of Wisconsin.

2. Filmstrip of dancers (modern dance), filmstrip of one-act play or short play.

3. Records of electronic music, classical music, jazz, etc.

4. Poetry. Pass out e.e.cummings poems for children to read. Also, have them hear a recording of some poetry.

Procedure

Have electronic music on when children come into the room. After everyone is there, begin discussion by asking children to identify what they heard. Ask: What does it sound like? Is it a form of music? Could it have been put together 100 years ago? Why not? Does it *express* something about our times? How does it make you feel?

Then go into a general discussion of feelings/moods: how we all have them, and that artists in the various fields of music, visual arts, and writing try to express them. Tell children that during the next few weeks they will be looking at, hearing, and reading different ways some people have found to express their feelings about themselves, things they have seen, or the feelings they think other people have.

Extend this experience for the gifted and those who are showing a sustained interest. Stage a "happening" (a structured environment) for the class. Have it project a specific mood or feeling. Plan with a group of three or four interested students, and have them choose a few moods to project to the class. Allow them to select their own media — music, filmstrips, or slides; change the seating structure of the room; cover the walls, put up big screens of artwork; have an action (pantomime play); or anything else they can think of. Be sure to allow time for a discussion afterwards.

Creating Self-Portraits by Cutting and Folding Paper[5]

Small children in grades one through three will have a fine art experience by creating self-portraits from paper.

Have pencils, paper, scissors, and glue ready. Put up mirrors or have a few hand mirrors available for use.

First, the children will feel their own faces to get the basic shapes. Then they will fold the paper in half and try to cut out a shape to match theirs. They can draw eyes and mouths to match what they feel with their fingers. Then, they will fold paper and cut noses and hair, which they will glue to the faces.

---

[5] Laura Joseph, B.S. Degree Art Ed., University of Wisconsin.

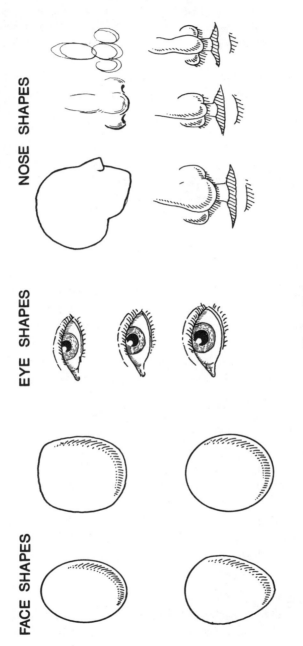

Figure 5-1

Second, pupils will make another self-portrait in the same way. This time, instead of feeling their own faces, they will look at them, using mirrors, as they cut out and draw their faces. Children will take turns using the mirrors, checking their work occasionally.

This activity will be fun, so tolerate some laughter and noise. However, promptly discourage disparaging remarks by children about their own or others' faces.

Youngsters aged five to ten will learn a great deal, as they enjoy constructing with paper. Use *Paper Construction for Children*[6] as a simple guide with detailed illustrations. Children can learn to construct people, animals, buildings, a tugboat, totem poles, puppets, and many other fascinating objects, using this easy-to-follow book.

Figure Drawing with Models

Figure drawing is an excellent activity for all sixth grade and junior high students. Children can use charcoal or pencils and inexpensive large newsprint paper, as they will want to make many impressions of the figure.

Select two or three children to serve as models for small groups. If you break up the large group the models will not be embarrassed. Ask them to wear fitted shirts or blouses and shorts, and have them stand on sturdy stools or chairs. Use caution in selecting your models, by avoiding the very beautiful or the very ugly. But, most important of all, do not choose restless children who cannot stand still for a while.

To begin with, you may wish a simple pose showing no movement. Next, for variety, have your models pose as if they were throwing a ball. It will be very challenging to draw.

Gifted and interested students may want to continue drawing more poses if there is time. Encourage them to keep sketch pads

---

[6] Norman Krinsky and Bill Berry, *Paper Construction for Children* (New York: Van Nostrand Reinhold Company, © 1966).

and charcoal handy at all times. They can make their own opportunities to draw, once you get them started.

How to Make a Diorama

A diorama is a good device to use for giving children various art experiences while they also do research in social studies. For example, if the class is studying pioneer life in early America, they can learn all about the way the pioneers lived, and then they can practice and display their new learning by planning and making a diorama. Children can use shoe boxes without covers, and they can construct cardboard figures, or model clay or papier-mâché figures (the best way), sew appropriate costumes for the period, and build or model miniature furniture and other artifacts. Pupils can read books, look at pictures, and go to museums to learn about the kind of homes and furniture that most of the pioneers had in different parts of the country.

The type of region that children study would lead them to special kinds of houses. If they are learning about a forested region, their diorama will either show the inside of a log cabin or have a miniature log cabin in a forest setting. If they are studying a prairie region, their pioneers might live in a sod house, built with strips of sod stacked one upon the other. Children would paint the background (the three inside walls, top, and bottom of the box), or glue colored construction paper on it, to show the forest or plains. If the outside surface of the shoe box has writing on it, this would have to be covered with construction paper.

The interior of the diorama will need furniture and people. For the correct furnishings, encyclopedias and other reference books could be used for authenticity. A fireplace with logs piled by its side would be needed. Churns, cradles, spiders and kettles, fireplace cranes, spinning wheels, and looms could be constructed of papier-mâché or cardboard. Use a lump of Plasticine as a base for objects that might fall. Each member of the family (except the baby) can be shown doing some useful work: churning, whittling, cooking, mending, spinning, or making candles and pouring them into molds.

Any kind of cloth, knitted fabric, wallpaper, or wood can be used for the diorama. If the kinds of materials are kept open, the necessity of choice will stimulate your pupils' creativity. They may think of something they have at home, or they may wish to knit or crochet a rug or wall hanging, or build some furniture from toothpicks and glue.

Dioramas require a great deal of time to plan and make. For suggestions on planning this time, you may wish to read the section on "Dioramas" in *Successful Techniques for Teaching Elementary Language Arts.*[7]

Suggestions for Creating a Pipe Cleaner City

This project was even more ambitious than it appeared. Robin and Gail,[8] two bright ten-year-olds, helped me build a pipe cleaner city. None of us had ever done anything like it before. The materials were clay, pipe cleaners, papier-mâché, cardboard, toothpicks, paper, and a flat box top.

We began with the flat box top and cut off two of its sides. Gail drew pictures of buildings on the inside surfaces of the two remaining sides. We started with a base of clay high enough to support our pipe cleaner buildings. It wasn't a good idea, because we didn't have enough clay to continue. The buildings with the high bases looked well, so we carved steps on two sides of each one. Gail fashioned buildings of various heights out of the pipe cleaners, attaching the four sides to four small pieces for the roof by twisting the pieces around each other. We made the mistake of starting out with some used pipe cleaners. They were too crooked and wobbly, no matter how hard we tried to straighten them. It was fun smoothing streets and sidewalks out of the clay.

---

[7] Rosalind Minor Ashley, *Successful Techniques for Teaching Elementary Language Arts* (West Nyack, N.Y.: Parker Publishing Company, Inc., 1970), pp. 211-12.
[8] Robin Procunier and Gail Carmichael; Glenview, Illinois.

Figure 5-2

One of the buildings became a church, with four pieces coming to a point on top, and a cross attached at the very top. The second time we did it, it looked better, because all four pieces were equal in length. (We folded two pipe cleaners in half evenly.)

We worked on this project at odd times, whenever one of the girls could come over, and we used whatever materials we had. Since we were now out of clay, Robin and I made a kind of putty out of 3 cups of flour, 2 cups of salt, and 1 cup of water. It was messy, but fun. We finally decided that the putty might work better with strips of newspaper added to the mixture with more water. It now became papier-mâché. We hoped that it would have more body and that it would mold easier. We made an expressway with an entrance ramp. Robin and I weren't sure that anyone would recognize it as an expressway, so we put a few toy cars on it. It still didn't look very much like an expressway, so Robin got the idea of using a Magic Marker to draw lane lines down the road. That helped.

We put doors in some of the buildings on two sides, and Robin built a TV antenna for one building. Our skyscraper collapsed because it wasn't strong enough, so we cut off pieces on all four sides and rebuilt it. All of the buildings needed extra support near all four bases.

One of our buildings had a large billboard suspended above it. Before the billboard was attached to its support, Gail and I both laughed at it because it looked more like a chair than a building. We made billboards out of cardboard, drew advertising pictures, and wrote slogans on them. Gail helped with this. "VERMONT KINGS — THE CIGARETTE FOR YOU!" and "YUM YUM — BUY SOUPO" were a few. We glued one billboard onto the building with putty. It kept coming off, but we kept sticking it back on. Robin thought that billboards near the expressway would fill up some of the empty spaces. We had a terrible time getting the billboards to stand up, but we solved the problem (temporarily) by propping them up with toothpicks.

The girls and I agreed that our city was O.K., but it would have been much better and easier to work with if we had used clay and only new pipe cleaners. We also decided that we had enjoyed building it.

Using Collage

Collages are so completely different from drawings and paintings that they provide not only variety, but an excellent artistic outlet for those who cannot **draw** or paint well. Encourage all of your pupils to try collage, but not until you show them the tremendous range of materials and subjects that they can use.

Try to provide a large assortment of supplies for collage. Once the children realize that "anything goes," some will be making collages at home and raiding their mother's pantry and sewing box to bring things in for their school creations. Use your imagination, and encourage children to use theirs. Anything that can be glued, sewed, or stapled to paper, wallpaper, or cloth can be collage material. For a background, you may supply colored construction paper or a piece of wallpaper. (Most wallpaper stores are happy to give away old wallpaper sample books.)

Your collage materials will suggest ideas for the collage itself. The wallpaper pattern may inspire unusual materials to attach. For example, there was a piece of humorous wallpaper showing a French poodle having its hair and nails done in a ladies' beauty shop. The poodle suggested tiny pieces of very old Persian lamb, which I glued to the appropriate spots on the picture of the poodle. Old scraps of fur, cloth, paper, magazines, valentines, or other greeting cards make wonderful materials. Use buttons, macaroni, rice, sand, sandpaper, yarn, plastic cartons, toothpicks, or pipe cleaners. A plastic tomato carton suggested a bridge to me, so I used one side of it for a bridge. I drew a funny little man who was walking on the edge of the railing of the bridge, balancing himself with a stirrer. His clothing was made of cloth, and a cloud in the sky above was made of cotton. The water beneath him came from a magazine ad. In one collage, there was a sketch of a girl on a match stick balcony talking to a man below her. The man held a guitar. (This was a wallpaper picture.) Another collage came from a magazine cartoon of Lady Godiva, which was completed by gluing human hair on her head that covered her entire body. Old packing material can give you suggestions. Some gifts came wrapped in brown wrinkled paper, which I saved. To go with this, I used brown cloth, sandpaper, corrugated paper, and other brown objects with various textures. It was fun to imagine what else to use. But the brown wrapping material got me started, and it ended up in an interesting abstract design with unusual textures. One newspaper picture of a bird with eggs in a nest started me off gluing straw on the picture of the nest, and it looked very real. A magazine picture of a gorilla got me going on a jungle scene with all sorts of green paper and cloth for foliage. To finish it off, I glued real leaves at the side. Very exotic. Another picture of a little boy sawing wood suggested wood shavings and a piece of wood, which I glued under the picture of the workbench. A black-and-white newspaper picture of a bull inspired a background of a red cloth cape and red cloth eyes for the bull. A magazine picture of a New Year's Eve celebration demanded (and got) rolls of confetti glued on it. Very festive! A picture of a little girl holding a tennis racket required a tennis net in the background. It came from some coarse netting in a bag that held onions.

Encourage children to combine drawing and painting with collage. A water color, tempera, or colored chalk background can be very effective.

Suggest two-and three-dimensional collages for those who have already made simple ones. Folded paper that seems to jump out from the page can make delightful jack-in-the-boxes. One collage that was interesting to make took two pages of materials. The background page was smooth silver foil. The top page was a pattern made of three colors of construction paper in a free-form design. There were holes cut in the design so that you could see the silver background through the holes.

If you want to have letters or words on your collage, or if you wish a title in collage form, you can use letters from a newspaper headline, a piece of newspaper, toothpicks, cloth, a rubber band, braid, ribbon, match sticks, or spaghetti.

Your collage may need a face. Buttons for eyes and yarn for a mouth or hair will be interesting. Red ribbon can make a good mouth.

You may get an idea that you wish to carry out in a unified way. One collage was titled "Killing Time," in letters cut from a timetable. Assorted pictures of clocks were arranged in a design; some wallpaper, some magazine or newspaper pictures. One large clock face was featured, with a toothpick dagger stabbing it. A face that came from an old watch was also in the design.

Some materials can produce interesting effects. Colored-paper cupcake liners can look like fans, pleated skirts, or accordians. Used film makes an interesting design. A shaggy dog can be created from brown yarn. A piece of coral against a marine-type background can be very beautiful. (You will have to stitch it on with a large needle. The stitches will show on the back.) Cut up an egg carton, as it can provide anything from abstract textured designs to figures of women.

Display your completed collages, and use collages for anything from bulletin boards to advertisements of school functions. Students can let their imaginations run wild with collage, because it frees them from the limitations of what they are able to draw.

Making a Research Mural

The research mural is much more than a social studies project that uses art to summarize its findings. It is a cooperative group activity that should be planned and carried out by students.

The best way to time a research mural is to have its planning start about ten days after the class has begun a social studies unit. Since the mural takes such a long time to plan, discuss, study for, sketch, and draw, if you wait too long interest will lag, and by then students will be studying another topic.

Let's say that a sixth grade class has begun its study of ancient Greece. There has been textbook reading and some class discussion. That is the time to divide the class into groups to study various aspects of life in the Greece of those days. It is too soon to discuss what the mural will contain. There may be groups studying the agriculture, the philosophers, the Persian wars, the famous buildings, the classes of people in a city-state like Athens, the gymnasiums, etc.

After some study by each group, reports could be given to share the research findings, and then plans could be made for the mural. The time is right to discuss the mural, as the class has now had enough background information to make choices, but not so much that they're bored with the subject. The teacher or a class leader can take suggestions from the group on what parts of early Greek life they want to show, and write them on the board for everyone to see.

The list of mural topics could possibly be:

Greek warships in the Aegean Sea
the Olympic Games
the Oracle at Delphi
the Parthenon on the Acropolis
a Greek home with its open courtyard
men and women wearing flowing tunics and cloaks
Greek farmers harvesting grapes and olives in the fall
a famous philosopher teacher with male pupils

Decisions will have to be made as to whether the group shows Delphi or the Acropolis at Athens. Also, whether to show Athens or the sea, which is 5 miles away at Piraeus. Great care must be taken to show the farms on plains in a ring around the hilly city, and not in it. As these choices are made, students will consolidate what they have learned, and they will become motivated to fill in the gaps in their knowledge.

Once the tentative mural subjects have been chosen, assign different groups to study each one for the purpose of drawing them correctly. Use sketches that are in good scale relative to each other. Cut the sketching paper to the same proportion as the dimensions of the mural paper — about 6-by-30-inch paper. Decide on a standard height for people and buildings to avoid difficulty later. Try to select at least one capable artist in each group.

Once the sketches are ready, have them put together on the floor in a rough plan of placement for the mural. This should certainly bring about much discussion and many changes. Look for constructive suggestions. Squelch the inevitable insulting comments on lack of artistic ability.

After that, have students put up a room-wide piece of 30-inch white paper. Assign definite spaces for small groups for every few yards of paper. This is an absolute necessity, or children will be crowding each other and drawing one thing right on another. Expect the first mural drawings to be done *lightly* in pencil or with pale yellow chalk. The reason for this is the necessity for many changes as the work progresses. If the first sketches are easy to change, the whole project will move smoothly.

Have many meetings before the mural is put in final form, and let the students decide what medium to use. Each has its own hazards, as colored chalk smears and powders off on the floor and paint runs. Colored chalk works well if you place newspaper on the floor to catch the colored chalk dust. Spray a fixative on each section as it is done, in order to minimize smearing. When the finished mural is drawn with colored chalk, or is painted, the students may wish to give it extra dimension with collage effects. This will challenge the students' creativity, as the pictures alone will suggest suitable materials to glue or staple on.

In this activity for the entire class, you will find that the students who are gifted in artistic ability will do a greater amount of drawing and painting than the others. They will be working at it in all of their spare time. The other children will admire their skill and ask them for help and advice.

The Piper Leads the Way — a Core Curriculum

One fifth grade teacher turned an old story into a core curriculum.[9] Her class adapted The Pied Piper of Hamelin into a play, doing all of the writing.

The students used encyclopedias to research the period for the village scenery and the costumes. They created their own scenery from packing cartons, and they used mathematics to measure perspective for it. Then the children painted the scenery with tempera paints. They stuffed colored stockings for the rats and pulled them on roller skates to get movement. Pupils painted pipe cleaners and attached them to the rats' bodies for tails. After they studied the period, the children drew sketches and then sewed their own costumes.

Students planned and created their own music, dances, and play programs. The children composed the songs for the play and danced to the piper, creating their own dance after learning how to do a few steps. The piper used a Flutaphone for the music. He had never played the instrument before, but he improvised his own tunes as he went along. The youngsters also produced their own play programs with color duplicating paper.

So, while planning and creating a dramatic performance, the class worked with many different subjects. They built their curriculum around their play.

The Michelangelo Ceiling Society — a Club

A special club for pupils who are talented or who have a strong interest in the arts could possibly include most of the children in your class. This does not mean that the club should be used as a catch-all for anyone who won't fit in any of the other clubs. It just works out that way if enough variety is explored.

---

[9] Ruth Ann Hodnett, Research Specialist and Consultant in Reading; Clarendon Hills, Illinois.

If the name of the club relates to painting, that does not mean that this is the only activity. Members can have interests in sculpture, collage, ceramics, paper construction, copper enameling, classical symphonies, opera, jazz, creative dramatics, ballet, modern dance, poetry, drama, fiction, and many other of the arts.

Schedule visits to art museums and concerts if possible. Invite artists of all kinds to come to display their talents. The club may want to invite a classmate or a teacher to perform, whether it is to sing, give a dramatic presentation, or play the guitar. Have workshops in various art forms, so that interested students can try some activities that they've never done before.

Broaden the members' appreciations as well as their knowledge of the arts. Once they know something about an art form, children will enjoy it more.

Some very useful materials for class and individual use are "Sound Slidesets." One set is on "Italian Baroque Art."[10] Another kit is called "19th Century Developments in Art."[11] Each kit includes a set of color slides, a 33-1/3 rpm LP record which gives a commentary, and a booklet with information on each slide, and a bibliography. There are many different kits to select from.

"New Sounds in Music" is a color film that presents new sounds and new ways of treating old sounds.[12] Chance music, tape music, synthesizer music, and other 20th century approaches to music are heard. In a mountain meadow, we hear "spontaneous sound" played on 100 or more gongs and other percussion instruments. In a rehearsal hall, experiments are done with chance music and group improvisation. You hear newly invented string and percussion instruments, two Bukla synthesizers, and sounds from a bulldozer. The intent of the film is to show that today's world of music is rich in varieties of sound and invention of forms.

---

[10] "Italian Baroque Art," SVE Sound Slideset, SL 103 SR. Society for Visual Education, Inc., 1345 Diversey Parkway, Chicago, Illinois 60614. ©MCMLXIX.

[11] "19th Century Developments in Art," SVE Sound Slideset, SL 107 SR. Society for Visual Education, Inc., 1345 Diversey Parkway, Chicago, Illinois 60614. ©MCMLXIX.

[12] "New Sounds in Music," 22 minutes, color, Primary-Intermediate, Churchill-Wexler Film Productions, 801 N. Seward St., Los Angeles, Calif.

Accompanying this film is a 10-inch LP record. It supplies additional listening material for classroom use after the film has been shown. The selections on it are not likely to be found in the school library. They will be excellent as examples for discussion and as a point of departure for creative projects in music.

Upper elementary, junior high, and high school students will enjoy hearing some of the different kinds of jazz music. Bring in a variety of these records to play at meetings. Play Dixieland jazz, and the music of some of the combos like the Oscar Peterson Quartet, the Ramsey Lewis Trio, and Miles Davis. Ramsey Lewis' "The 'In' Crowd" is a jazz classic that would make an excellent first experience with jazz.[13] If you are a jazz fan, bring some of your own favorite records or tapes. Your enthusiasm will help the group to enjoy the music even more.

Some interested students might then like to read how jazz got started, and where. They'll enjoy learning about the careers of some of our jazz greats. *Cool, Hot and Blue; A History of Jazz for Young People* will make good reading.[14]

The club may wish to listen to one of the many fine recordings of poetry for one meeting. The poems will be doubly enjoyed if you allow students to experience the poem visually while they hear it. Make up an overhead visual of the poem and display it on an overhead projector.

A great way to learn about and enjoy a play is to have a play reading. Duplicate copies of a selected play, assign parts, and read it aloud informally, sitting in a circle. The reading will go more smoothly if you allow time before you start for each member to circle in red the parts he is to read aloud. If you wish to repeat the play, it will add interest for everyone if the parts and circled scripts are switched. After the play reading, have the club president lead a discussion about the play. Give him a few guidelines: What kind of a play is this? What was the playwright

[13] "The 'In' Crowd," *The In Crowd*, The Ramsey Lewis Trio, Side One, Band One. LP-757, Cadet. Chess Producing Corp., Chicago, Illinois 60616.

[14] Charles Boeckman, *Cool, Hot and Blue; A History of Jazz for Young People* (Washington, D.C.: Robert B. Luce, Inc., 1968).

trying to say? What mood did the play inspire? Does this play remind you of any other well-known play? Did the characters seem real? Why?

You will probably have more suggestions for meetings than you need. In case you all run dry of ideas, a fine book that can suggest activities for meetings (and lessons) is *What Can I Do for an Art Lesson?; A Practical Guide for the Elementary Classroom Teacher.*[15]

CHECKLIST

Realize that talent in the arts is probably more widespread and more difficult to identify than any other kind.

Avoid tests, as there are no satisfactory tests for identifying talent in the fine arts.

Use experts to judge talent in the arts.

Assume some talent if you observe a combination of outstandingly beautiful or original creations, as well as extreme perseverance and interest.

Look for reorganization of a subject in a work of art, as this is considered better than realistic work.

Use the arts as an unequalled opportunity for finding an activity in which a child can excel.

Search for the talented by providing variety of expression, rather than by trying to identify them.

Stimulate upper-grade students by having them complete a painting that has been partially obscured.

Teach students that the arts can express the feelings of the artist, or they can establish a mood.

Have young children create self-portraits from paper.

Use students as models for figure drawing.

Combine a social studies unit and art by having students make authentic dioramas of an historic period.

---

[15] Ruth L. Peck and Robert S. Aniello, *What Can I Do for an Art Lesson?; A Practical Guide for the Elementary Classroom Teacher* (West Nyack, New York: Parker Publishing Company, Inc., 1966).

Have pupils build a city from pipe cleaners.

Use new pipe cleaners and a clay base for the pipe cleaner city.

Encourage all children to try collage, which is an excellent artistic outlet for those who cannot draw or paint well.

Get ideas for collage from the materials you use.

Plan and carry out a class research mural.

Use a research mural as a group activity that teaches social studies, art, research skills, and group cooperation.

Allow a long time for the planning, research, sketching, and drawing of a research mural.

Expect some knowledge of the subject before decisions and sketches are made.

Have mural sketches made on paper that is 6 by 30 inches, so that sketches will match the mural paper.

Decide on a standard height for people and buildings, so that sketches will be in proportion to each other.

Assign spaces for work on the final mural, so that children won't get in each other's way or ruin someone else's drawing.

Do the first mural drawings in light yellow chalk or lightly pressed pencil, so that changes will be easy to make.

Permit students to make the decisions on subject matter to be drawn, sketches to be chosen, and the medium to be used.

Use a play as a core curriculum to teach writing, dancing, painting, songwriting, research skills, social studies, mathematics, sewing, etc.

Include any child who shows talent or interest in a special club for the arts.

Vary the club's activities to include every type of handiwork, collage, painting, drawing, art and music appreciation, study of music and instruments, dramatics, dancing, and the appreciation and creation of literature.

Ideas for Pupils
Who Are Bright
in Science

Chapter Six

T he bright child will get more out of an experiment or demonstration if he plans it himself. The ideal situation is seldom achieved, but you can aim for it. In this case, the child gets curious about something and designs his own experiment. When this happens, you don't have to motivate him. Your only problem will be getting him to stop — for anything — recess, lunch, gym, or going home.

One possible way to arouse this sense of wonder and curiosity, that can lead to meaningful experiments, is by having a constant new supply of raw materials and data for the child to wonder about. A permanent science table is a wonderful thing — if the *exhibit* isn't permanent too. Autumn leaves are fine for a few days, but when they begin to get dusty, they've been there much too long. It's not enough to settle for the occasional grasshopper or seashell that pupils bring in. The science materials room is a fine source, as well as the district Materials Center, if you have one. If you have nothing new of value to display, throw away or save the old exhibits and put up a temporary film loop projector with a selection of science film loops. Or borrow a filmstrip previewer from the library and provide a variety of filmstrips.

An ant farm or a fish tank can be stimulating for primary grade pupils, especially if they are displayed for a few weeks only. Share them with other classes. When they're in the classroom too long, they're ignored. Don't limit yourself to displays on just the one unit you're studying, but put up anything of possible interest. It could be a group of microscopes with slides.

Many times an experiment is performed by one child and the rest of the children never get a chance to look closely at it. After some experiments are done, leave the materials out so that anyone interested can try them out too. Naturally, you would avoid leaving out anything dangerous like gas burners or most chemicals. In many cases, children don't really learn too much from observing an experiment. They need to try it out themselves. The best science exhibit I ever had in my third grade classroom was a collection of rocks that the children could test, some vinegar, and some files, glass, and a penny. (I hid the hammer and knife.)

Another great display was a glass tank half-filled with water, and the various plastic cups, siphons, and other materials for experimenting with air pressure. Admittedly, the science area was a bit damp, but the children thought it was worth it. A truly fine science table is a messy one that's being *used*.

If the child is going to do an experiment that is already planned, it should be related to a question of his or something he is actively working on and curious about. He can get more involved in it if he gathers (or brings from home), the necessary equipment and materials. Give him time and space, and only whatever help is necessary. He needs the stimulation of getting everything ready, of measuring things, heating or cooling objects, and making the charts on the board. This is not busy work, but an integral part of *his* experiment. It will not mean much to a bright child to do someone else's experiment, to answer someone else's question, with materials that have been gathered and prepared by the teacher. He'll think it's the *teacher's* experiment and will not get emotionally involved in it. He might act so sluggish by then that the teacher actually has to help him through it.

Gifted children are stimulated by laboratory equipment, as all children usually are, but it is more important to emphasize the thinking up of good questions and hypotheses rather than the manipulation of materials.

Good science education relates scientific discoveries with mankind and how men use an invention for good or evil. It relates science to local and world problems.

Good science work requires a child to put in effort. It also helps him to try again after a failure, after he understands the reasons for it. The gifted child should be expected to go into his assignments in more depth than other pupils. The average child may demonstrate a concept. The bright one will do this, *plus* figure out a way to use it.

This chapter will give some clues to finding children talented in science. It will tell how to role-play the planets, and how to build an erosion model of the earth. You will learn how to conduct an Insect Hunt, and how to prepare your own terrarium. Some possible ideas for helping children with Science Fair projects are given, as well as tactful ways to keep parents interested, but not let them take over. You will find out how one gifted child made brownies out of algae. Possible ideas for a science club are also suggested.

Finding the Talented

A child who has ability in science will give you hints of it. He will seek out books and filmstrips about insects, microscopes, rocks, outer space, etc., and he will ask questions about scientific topics. This child will show interest by collecting butterflies, fossils, or shells, and he will bring many objects of scientific interest into the classroom. In discussions of current events, he will concentrate on new cures for diseases, inventions, and scientific events. His interest will show itself in better attention during science lessons than at other times. He may have keen observation, attention to detail, and the patience to watch and wait. He will volunteer to do experiments and possibly tell of some he has tried out at home. On museum field trips, he will want to spend more time at scientific exhibits than you can spare. He will keep touching and examining objects at the science table (often at the wrong times).

This *continued* interest in science, and mathematical talent, are big factors in indentification of ability. High scores in achievement tests in science are also good indicators.

Outdoor Orbits — What to Do When Role-Playing the Planets

Before you do this planet demonstration, set up a model of the solar system in the classroom.[1] Allow the children who are participating in the activity to have special time to look at and manipulate the model — possibly more time than you might ordinarily allow. They will get much more out of the entire experience if they have an opportunity to get very familiar with the physical model, to study the various sizes of the planets and their different distances from the earth.

Role-playing the planets will be an excellent science activity for an entire fourth grade class to participate in.[2] Give the measuring and timing responsibilities to four children who are gifted in science.

Objectives: Students can: 1. Play the roles of nine planets revolving around the sun, walking around it at approximate relative distances.

2. State that the farther a planet is from the sun, the longer it takes to make a complete revolution around the sun.

Materials: tape measure

chalk

2 stopwatches

Procedure: 1. Assign the roles of nine planets and the sun to ten children. Choose two gifted pupils to do the measuring and two to do the timing.

2. Show a demonstration model of our solar system so that pupils can see the relative distances of the planets from the sun.

3. Discuss what would make a logical and usable scale of miles so that the proportionate distances could be measured on the schoolyard. Use 1 inch = 1 million miles for your chart, shown in Figure 6-1.

---

[1] "Solar System," T.N. Hubbard Scientific Co., Northbrook, Ill.

[2] *"Sun, Moon and Planets,"* Science Curriculum, Grade Four, 1966. The Wilmette Public Schools, District #39, Wilmette, Illinois.

Planet (arranged in order from the sun)	Approximate Distance from Sun (mills. of miles)	Distance on the School-yard (feet)	Time for Orbit (minutes)
Mercury	36	3	
Venus	67	6	
Earth	93	8	
Mars	141	12	
Jupiter	483	41	
Saturn	886	74	
Uranus	1783	149	
Neptune	2792	232	
Pluto	3666	309	

Figure 6-1

4. Write the incomplete chart on the board.

5. Find an open spot on the schoolyard.

6. Two children will use the chart to mark off on the ground the distances from the "sun" for the nine "planets" to stand on.

7. Have the nine "planets" place themselves on the marked spots.

8. The "planets" will walk at the same pace around the stationary "sun," keeping in their orbits, for a practice walk, and then stop.

9. The two timekeepers will give a signal and the "planets" will walk in orbit again. They will clock the time it takes for each "planet" to walk once around the "sun" from the marked starting place. This might take a while, as they will have to clock two planets at a time.

10. After the orbiting, the timekeepers will write the orbit time for each "planet" on the chart on the board.

11. Ask the two pupils who did the measuring to lead a discussion about the project. Allow the children to discover from the completed chart that the farther the planet is from the sun, the longer it takes to make a complete revolution. Encourage the leaders to formulate their own questions. If they need help, give the leaders questions like:

What did you learn from the timing of the orbits?
How long did it take for Pluto to orbit?
How far is Pluto from the sun?
How long did it take Mercury to orbit?
How far is Mercury from the sun?

Try to have the children themselves summarize what they have learned.

This activity will start out as one class's project, but don't be surprised if you have a large audience from other classes before your practice orbit walk is over. This is the kind of activity that will appeal to children. Once a child has been "Saturn" or "Jupiter," he will be more likely to remember how these planets relate to the sun. Even more important, you will find a high interest in learning more about the solar system.

Have the children take an imaginary trip through space. In planning their trip, discuss such questions as:

1. Which object would you come to first; that is, what natural body is closest to the earth? (moon)

2. Take a "ride" to the closest planet. Which one would that be? (Venus)

3. If you traveled at 25,000 miles per hour, how long would it take you to get to the moon? (If it is about 240,000 miles away, it would take about ten hours.)

Allow children to select one planet for independent research and a report. Important facts that they can look for are:

1. Size.

2. Atmosphere.

3. Temperature.

4. Satellites.

5. Rotation.

6. Revolution.

7. Orbit.

8. Force of gravity.

9. Possibility of life.

10. Unusual features (i.e., Saturn's rings).

Present the film "A Trip to the Planets."[3] It shows an imaginary trip to the planets, with models demonstrating composition and structure of the solar system, giving the size and appearance of the planets. The film explains how the sun produces its enormous energy.

An excellent record to go with this activity is "Space Songs."[4] Encourage pupils to take notes on the record if they can. You will want to repeat it many times.

Some Ways to Build an Erosion Model

One simple way to build an erosion model is given below:

Objectives: The pupil can demonstrate that:
1. Water erodes topsoil, leaving rocks.
2. Different kinds of soil erode at different rates.

Materials: 1 aluminum foil pie pan with holes punched in the bottom.
5 bottle caps or small rocks
some fine black topsoil (enough to fill pan)
some solid clay soil (enough to fill pan)
some water, in a large sprinkling can
a stopwatch
a very large dishpan (bigger than the pie pan)

Procedure: Place the bottle caps or small rocks in the pie pan. Fill the pan with fine, black topsoil packed down solidly. Place the pie pan in a large dishpan. Mark down the time. Then sprinkle the pie pan, simulating rain. Time how long it takes to wash away half of the topsoil, leaving bottle caps or rocks showing. Time how long it takes to wash away all of the topsoil.

Questions to ask:

What happened? (The topsoil eroded and was washed away through the holes in the pan.)

---

[3] "A Trip to the Planets" — 15 minutes, No. 1996, Encyclopaedia Britannica Educational Corp. Film Library, 1822 Pickwick Ave., Glenview, Illinois 60025.
[4] Tom Glazer, "Space Songs," Motivation Records 0312.

What was left? (The bottle caps or rocks.)

How long did it take to wash away half of the topsoil? (The time varies.)

How long did it take to wash away all of the topsoil? (The time varies.)

Now fill the pie pan with clay soil packed down solidly. Repeat the sprinkling and timing procedures.

Questions to ask:

What happened? (Some of the clay soil eroded and was washed away through the holes in the pan.)

How long did it take to wash away half of the clay soil? (The time varies.)

How long did it take to wash away all of the clay soil? (The time varies. The children may stop timing this before all of the clay is eroded.)

Did one of the soils erode faster than the other? (Yes.)

Which soil eroded faster? (Fine, black topsoil.)

Another type of erosion model that can be built is one that illustrates the relationship between slope and erosion.

Objectives: The child can demonstrate that:

1. Water will erode topsoil.

2. Topsoil on a high slope erodes faster than topsoil on a low slope.

Materials:

2 shoeboxes or wooden boxes with one narrow end cut off

enough aluminum foil to line boxes and make spouts

enough fine, black topsoil to fill both boxes

some water, in a large sprinkling can

2 pails

a stopwatch

a very large pan (big enough to hold 2 pails)

Procedure: Line both boxes with aluminum foil, making a pouring spout at one narrow end of each box. Set boxes on the edge of a table. Raise the closed end of one box 1 inch. (You can use books or pieces of wood to raise the boxes.) Raise the closed end of the other box 4 inches.

Place the two pails in a large pan under the box spouts so that they can collect all runoff. Sprinkle each box with the same amount of water.

Time the runoff for 15 minutes. Observe the amount and color of the runoff. Time it for another half hour and observe runoff. Time it after another hour. Observe and measure runoff.

Questions to ask:

Did the water erode the topsoil? (Yes.)

Which box had the most erosion? (The one with the high slope.)

If you wish to figure the per cent of slope, *Teaching Elementary Science: A Sourcebook for Elementary Science* has a lesson that helps you to do it.[5]

You may vary this erosion model by having different kinds of soil in each box, having harder, heavier rainfall in one box, or covering the topsoil in one box with a sod cover.

Planning an Insect Hunt

This activity, which is great for the entire class, will be a catalyst for your pupils who have talent in science. It will lead them into collecting, research, and intensive study.

Plan an Insect Hunt in May, June, or early September, unless you have insects available all winter. It is an organized collecting of specimens for study. The children will also think of it as a wonderful outing. If your school has a grassy area with bushes, this place would be fine. Otherwise, organize a field trip to a nearby park.

Objectives: The pupils will:

Collect insect specimens for study.

Make plans to start their own insect collections.

Begin studying insect life.

Materials: 20 or more plastic containers

---

[5] Elizabeth B. Hone, Alexander Joseph, and Edward Victor; *Teaching Elementary Science: A Sourcebook for Elementary Science* (New York: Harcourt Brace Jovanovich, Inc., 1962), pp. 120-21.

some large glass jars with nylon stockings over the openings

some rubber bands

some soil and leaves

two old sheets

some honey, molasses, or mashed bananas

2 ozs. rubbing alcohol

1 box of cotton

at least 2 tablespoonsful of Carbona (carbon tetrachloride)

2 round, jar-size cardboard pieces with several holes in them

some cigar boxes or wood boxes

some hosiery boxes with cellophane replacing most of the covers

some corrugated paper

some moth flakes

some pins (long, thin insect pins are best)

some broomsticks

some heavy wire or wire coat hangers

some heavy net curtains or cheesecloth

a small sponge

Procedure: 1. Help children make insect nets. Bend a wire into a circle about 40 cm. in diameter and twist the ends together to form a straight piece at least 15 cm. long. Staple the straight part of the wire to a broomstick, or tie it on with more wire. Cut cheesecloth in a pie shape to form a net about 75 cm. deep. Stitch it to the circular wire frame.

2. Prepare nylon-covered glass jars in the classroom with some soil and leaves at the bottom.

3. Have two killing jars ready with about an ounce of rubbing alcohol in each one — this will kill most insects, except butterflies and moths.

4. Have two killing jars ready with cotton saturated with at least 1 tablespoonful of carbon tetrachloride in each jar — for butterflies and moths. Cover the cotton with a round cardboard piece.

5. Get cigar boxes ready with corrugated paper or cotton in the bottom. (Pinning is easy with corrugated paper.)

6. Send children out hunting with plastic containers, sheets, and honey (or molasses, or mashed bananas).

Teach children how to collect insects. Suggest that they look carefully under large stones and logs. Tell them to spread a sheet out under a bush or in tall weeds. Then they will shake the bush or weeds and roll up the sheet quickly. Warn children to free all stinging insects and to use nets and tweezers rather than their hands. Have them open all the plastic boxes and be ready to catch the insects on the sheet as they slowly unroll it. Then they cover the boxes quickly. Some of the group will attract flies and ants by spreading honey, molasses, or mashed bananas in various spots, checking them at time intervals. Others will catch flying insects with nets, quickly transferring them to containers and covering them.

When the children have caught as many insects as possible, return to the classroom and transfer some of them to the nylon-covered glass jars. A few beetles, and ants may be dropped into alcohol killing jars. Moths and butterflies can be killed for collection by carefully putting them in wide-mouthed glass killing jars with cotton and carbon tetrachloride. (Warn children not to inhale the fumes.) Observe the live insects for a short while and let them free. Before you can mount the dead insects, relax them in a jar that has a small, damp sponge in it. Keep insects there until their bodies are flexible. Start your insect collection by removing the dead specimens, carefully pinning them in the cigar box lined with cotton or corrugated paper, and labelling them with names of insects and where you collected them. Place moth flakes in each insect box to protect the collection.

Insects with wide wings will mount better in a shallow hosiery box nearly filled with cotton, with a cover that has had its top replaced with cellophane. Use moth flakes for this box.

The Insect Hunt will lead directly into curiosity and research for all of the children. Your gifted pupils will be ready now for independent study.

No matter how many (or how few) insects your class collects, the hunt will be a memorable occasion, causing many children in other classes to be running about with insect nets for some time.

Single-concept film loops are valuable for individual and

small-group instruction. The main advantage of the film loop is the ease with which it can be used by the pupils themselves, with little possibility of their harming the material. Tell children not to remove the loop while the projector is turned on. There is a growing selection of film loops in many subject areas.

"Helpful Insects," which lasts for about four minutes, is one of the many science film loops available for third and fourth grade pupils.[6] It stresses a single concept — that some insects are helpful to man and nature.

Each film loop package gives much information, which the children should read. With the name and number, it tells the film time length, the concept, and anticipated student understanding. The film loop is described in detail, and suggested preview assignments and discussion topics are given. A film loop can be adapted for use with other levels by changing the preview assignments, discussion topics, and follow-up activities. Read aloud the package information for young children.

Studying Spiders

One subject that is sure to interest young science lovers is the study of spiders. The president of the National Arachnid Society has written a fascinating illustrated article about them.[7] The study of spiders might naturally come after your Insect Hunt, as some pupil is sure to bring you a spider and call it an "insect." This is your "teachable moment" when you can show him the difference between spiders and insects, and lead some children into independent study on spiders. The article will give you a great deal of help with this, pointing out the exact differences, and explaining and illustrating the seven stages of a spider's web.

The author tells how to collect spiders. The article identifies the dangerous black widow spider by its red hourglass marking on its underside. Because some people are highly allergic to spider

---

[6] "Helpful Insects," 81-401; International Communications Foundation, Ealing Film-Loops; Cambridge, Massachusetts 02140.

[7] Ann Moreton, President, National Arachnid Society; Powhatan, Virginia; "Spiders," *Science and Children,* Vol. 8, No. 1, September, 1970, 7-10.

venom, it is wise to show children how to use an insect net, a sieve, and a tweezers, rather than handle the spiders with their hands.

Spider enthusiasts can learn more about these interesting animals by joining The National Arachnid Society. The dues are six spiders annually, for which members receive a collecting sheet, *Spider Bulletin*, a membership card, and a newsletter.

You will find the magazine *Science and Children* a useful store of ideas for all of your science activities. It is attempting to convince all of its authors to adopt the metric system, and it will be valuable in helping you to teach your pupils to use it.

How to Create a Miniature Forest Floor

Good terrariums can be made in large (gallon-sized) jars, which may be obtained from school cafeterias or restaurants. The jars are not as easy to work with as the large glass aquariums that are open at the top. For display purposes, they may be held firm in wood holders. These can be made by nailing small strips of wood to a flat piece of wood.

If you use an aquarium, get a piece of glass a bit larger than the top and tape its edges to be used as a cover. An old, leaky aquarium can be useful this way.

Have pupils help you prepare the terrarium with a few pieces of charcoal in the bottom, some sand, and some damp forest soil. Use only enough soil to cover the roots of the plants completely. A small container buried in the soil can serve as a miniature lake and a source of moisture. Fill it after your soil is ready.

Be sure to get healthy plants that thrive in a damp forest environment. Small ferns, violets, baby tears, miniature ivy, and philodendrons will do well. You can purchase these plants in small pots. If you live in the country, you may find them growing wild. If your only possible source is a forest preserve, contact the people in charge and ask permission to take a few plants. They may allow you to take one of a kind from a few groups of plants. Take enough soil to cover the roots. Plant carefully, firming the soil in place around each plant, arranging the tallest plants in the corners or at the back. Sprinkle, and cover the terrarium.

The water from the "lake" will evaporate and fall as rain, providing a complete environment. If you keep the terrarium covered at all times, you will not need to water it.

Draw a plan of your miniature forest floor, numbering each plant. Have a key with this diagram, so that pupils can learn to identify the plants.

Having a Science Fair — Parent and Teacher Involvement

Science fairs for upper elementary students can be well worth the time and effort. Teams of teachers from all of the upper grades can do the planning of the fair and the motivating of students. Teachers and parents are usually willing to be available as a source of encouragement, supplies, and occasional suggestions. The actual planning and work of the exhibits must be done *by the students alone* for them to have any value. A *tactful* mimeographed sheet on this may be useful for informing parents.

One possible way to minimize parent involvement in science fair projects is to have all the planning and much of the project work done at school. Since all of your students will not be entering projects, regular class periods for this will be scarce. Encourage students to work at school, either before or after regular classes, or in study periods. Give them locked drawers or cabinets in which to store their projects and supplies.

You can make an important contribution in the planning of projects. Help students select projects that they can complete on their own. This means you can help each one decide, being realistic about his background, talents, sources of supplies, time and money available, and ability to stick to a project.

Once the projects are planned and under way, you must resist the temptation to do the thinking and work for the students. You, as a teacher, can become almost as emotionally involved as a parent in the success of a project. Be scrupulously fair in giving equal help to all participants. It is better for a student to start all over again on a simpler project than to have the work on his project shared by his teacher or parent.

Ideas for projects can come from units studied in school, or from a student's reading or hobbies. Sometimes class experiments or demonstrations suggest other, more complex investigations. The ideal project is one that can only be presented after new learning from a detailed study, original experiments, much research, or the building of new equipment. There is little learning involved when students make elaborate posters and displays about things they already know well. If a student wishes to display a hobby, such as ham radio equipment, encourage him to start a new project — perhaps build a new, more difficult set than the one he built before. Discourage the showing of previously built ham radio sets.

Ask students to collect the following materials around their homes for possible use in science or science fair projects:

cardboard boxes	corrugated boxes
small glass jars (baby food)	discarded clothing
small plastic bottles	clean tin cans (no sharp edges)
thin wire clothes hangers	pieces of wood
old toys	wire
pieces of metal	aluminum pans
batteries	

There are many ways of displaying a science project. A combination of color posters, with drawings, photographs, and hinged pegboard, can be very effective. Labelled photographs are good for showing changes in a specimen over a period of time. Data on graph paper can show changes, too. Molecule models can be made of plaster, painted, and glued on a poster. Metal holders and test tubes, vials, and Petri dishes can be combined with posters to dramatize an exhibit.

A scientifically written paper should describe the hypotheses, materials, procedures, and conclusions. All results should be recorded and explained.

The Illinois Junior Academy of Science, Inc., is an organization for junior and senior high school students interested in science.[8] Science clubs and schools register with it and compete for local, regional, and state honors on projects and scientific papers. Criteria for judging scientific papers are: scientific work

---

[8] Mr. David Curtis, State President, Illinois Junior Academy of Science, Inc.; North Chicago Community High School, North Chicago, Illinois 60064.

(including educational value, thoroughness, and difficulty) and comprehension. Outstanding and First Place winners are recommended to colleges and universities for scholarships.

Creating a Recipe from Algae

Green algae are dried and pressed into cakes to serve as food for man in coastal regions.[9]

This fact about algae was found in a fine science encyclopedia. It shows that algae has already been used as a source of food.

A teacher who taught fifth grade in Clearwater, Florida, tells of a student who used information read in an article about the food values of algae and how it might be used for human food. [10] The pupil planned it for her project in a science fair. She processed algae and she used it in a brownie recipe, adding it to all of the other ingredients. The brownies were delicious, and some of them were enjoyed at a class party. Everyone was skeptical at first, but pleasantly surprised, as no one could taste the algae in the brownies. When the brownies were entered in the science fair, they were awarded one of the prizes.

Edith Katherine Schuele, a 15-year-old high school senior from Memphis, Tennessee, told a Medical Association meeting that cookies can be made from algae.[11] She exhibited cookies, cinnamon pinwheels, French bread, and cheese swirls; all made from the green growth that floats on ponds. Algae is being considered as a food that could be grown aboard rocket ships for long space flights.

Edith said that she grew the algae, spun it in a centrifuge, and heated it. She obtained a powder that tastes like broccoli. When used in foods, algae increases the protein content by 20 % and the fat content by 75%.

In this way, two bright students conceived original experiments to find ways of increasing and improving our food supply.

---

[9] "Algae," *Young People's Science Encyclopedia,* (1962), I, 58-59.

[10] Ruth Ann Hodnett, Research Specialist and Consultant in Reading; Clarendon Hills, Illinois.

[11] "Spaceman's Dessert," *Science News Letter,* Vol. 75, No. 25, June 20, 1959, 387.

The Mad Scientists' Club

This club, especially for children interested and talented in science, will never run out of things to do. Youngsters of this type always have a project at hand or an experiment they want to try out. With a regular after-school (or before-school) time, your help with materials, and a group of fellow scientists, pupils will stimulate each other, leading one another into unexplored paths of science. A few experiments and demonstrations are suggested here. Any or all of them can be shared later with the class, after the club has practiced and discussed them.

For safety reasons, some adult should be present at all meetings. If you are there, but are busy and cannot help with the questions and answers or discussion after an experiment, try to brief the club president so that he is prepared to do it. With older students, this is preferable. The experiments can deteriorate into pointless games if the club members do not ask questions, perform experiments, and answer their questions afterwards.

Have members do an experiment. Then stimulate scientific thought by changing one of the conditions of the experiment and asking pupils, "What will happen now?"

There will also be times for just observation or "messing around" with materials. Pupils may be watching an ant farm, looking at other insects, studying various slides with microscopes, or examining objects with a hand lens. In such cases, even informal discussion is unnecessary.

One of the most popular experiments that was ever done in my class was making an egg pop into a bottle by using air pressure. Once your club members show this to the rest of the class, there will be an epidemic of egg popping. The wild interest in this experiment will almost justify the waste of so many eggs, and you'll all have a great deal of fun with it. This experiment is from *Teaching Elementary Science: A Sourcebook for Elementary Science.*[12]

> The children will enjoy watching you put a hard-boiled egg into a milk bottle. Obtain a small hard-boiled egg that is slightly larger than the

[12] Elizabeth B. Hone, Alexander Joseph, and Edward Victor, *Teaching Elementary Science: A Sourcebook for Elementary Science* (New York: Harcourt Brace Jovanovich, Inc., 1962), p. 139.

mouth of a milk bottle, and peel the egg. Make a twist of paper and light it with a match. While the paper is burning, drop it into the milk bottle and quickly set the peeled egg into the mouth of the milk bottle (Figure 6-2). Almost as soon as the flame goes out, the egg goes through the neck of the bottle with a loud pop.

Point out that the burning paper uses up some of the oxygen from the air in the bottle and also drives some of the air out through expansion. This means there is less air in the bottle and, consequently, less air pressure. The air pressure on the outside of the bottle is now greater than the air pressure inside the bottle. The air on the outside thus pushes the egg into the bottle.

To get the egg out of the bottle, tip the bottle mouth down so that the egg rests in the neck of the bottle. Lean your head all the way back and press the mouth of the bottle against your own mouth until it is airtight. Now blow hard into the bottle. This will force much air into the bottle until the air pressure inside the bottle is greater than the air pressure outside. The air inside will now push the egg out.

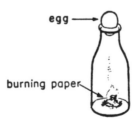

Making an egg pop into a bottle.

Figure 6-2

We were not always as successful at getting the egg out of the bottle as we were at getting it in. However, you may be able to save a few whole eggs.

A fine demonstration can be presented to the club members (and later the entire class) by one or two pupils, using "The

Talking Heart" materials.[13] These include a model of the human heart with numbered parts, some of which can be removed or moved. There is also a record and a booklet.

The booklet contains a key to the model and information on related visual aids. It also has diagrams of the heart and an exact script of the recording. There are suggestions for individual and class activities, using the model. It suggests related texts, film-strips, charts, models, transparencies, test sheets, and study guides. Related activities for extending uses of the model are also given.

You will get maximum effectiveness from this demonstration if you allow everyone in the class to handle and examine this model for at least a week before the event. The pupils who present the demonstration will need an even longer time, with some special time alone with the model to get familiar with each part — preferably before they hear the recording or read the script.

You will find *Science Activities* an interesting and challenging magazine for giving you ideas for club meetings. One article tells about a chemistry game with its modifications.[14] It is based on Scrabble.

> Elements are drawn randomly from the various chemical families and put into order to form equations (with appropriate coefficients)...The objective is to form chemical reactions which give valid compounds (as can be verified in the literature).

For the entire class, or younger club members (six through nine years old), the same magazine has an article with some science game ideas that will be very stimulating.[15] One activity pictured and described is a game called THINK, which is played very much like BINGO. It uses the letters T H I N K at the top of each card. The caller reads a call card.

---

[13] "The Talking Heart," Model 70140, with Record 62002. Denoyer-Geppert, 5235 Ravenswood Ave., Chicago, Illinois 60640.

[14] William Torop and John Joniac, "Games Chemistry Students Play," *Science Activities*, Vol. 5, No. 2, March, 1971, 11-12.

[15] Victor L. Weber, Jr., Albert P. Nous, and Robert N. Costa, "Science Learning Games in an Individualized Setting," *Science Activities*, Vol. 5, No. 2, March, 1971, 13-19.

For example, under the T: "I am used to keep track of short periods of time." Each student checks his card under the letter T. If the student has a picture of a sand timer under the letter T, he places a marker on the picture of the sand timer. Play continues until a player completes a horizontal, vertical, or diagonal line.

Another game that is pictured and described is called "Rally Race." It is played by two to four students. The game features various forms of metric measurement.

A "Space Game" for two to four students is pictured. In this game, children answer questions concerning solids, liquids, and gases.

Some examples of the game cards are given for these games, but the complete games are not covered in the articles; however, there is enough information given to get you started on creating your own games. Club members will enjoy composing cards for games and doing the research needed.

In most cases, members will share their activities with other class members, with great benefits for all.

CHECKLIST

Encourage children to originate and plan their own experiments.

Change classroom science exhibits often.

Involve children in experiments related to their questions and interests.

Allow pupils to prepare experiments themselves and to provide as many materials as possible.

Emphasize good questions and hypotheses rather than the manipulation of materials.

Relate scientific discoveries with mankind and how men use the inventions.

Require all children to put effort into their science work.

Expect extra depth from gifted pupils' work.

Have children try again after failures — after they understand the reasons for them.

Use a continued interest in science, mathematical talent, and high scores in science achievement tests as some indicators of ability in science.

Encourage observation and manipulation of a model solar system before you study the unit.

Teach the solar system by having pupils role-play the planets and take imaginary space trips.

Have children build various erosion models in order to understand erosion of soil and the effect of slope on erosion.

Stimulate study and hobbies about insects with the organized collecting of specimens in an Insect Hunt.

Emphasize safety: avoid or free all stinging insects, and use tweezers and insect nets for handling insects and spiders, rather than hands.

Free all insects that are not needed for study after you observe them for about a day.

Have pupils help you build a terrarium to simulate a forest floor.

Inform parents *tactfully* not to help students work on science fair projects.

Minimize parent involvements by having most of the science fair project work done at school.

Help students select realistic science fair projects that they can successfully plan and finish themselves.

Resist the temptation to help in more than the planning and supplies for science fair projects.

Give equal amounts of help and supplies to all science fair participants, if possible.

Suggest science fair projects that require new learning — from detailed study, much research, original experiments, or the building of new equipment.

Avoid projects that display material the student already knows.

Have the hypotheses, materials, procedures, and conclusions of each science fair project described in a student-written scientific paper that records and explains all results.

Provide a club for pupils who are interested and talented in science.

Be present at all meetings for safety reasons.

Help club members with questions and discussions about experiments, and teach the club president how to take over when possible.

Encourage students to plan and suggest ideas for projects at club meetings, and give suggestions when needed.

Use magazines to find ideas for club meetings.

Plan with club members to share most of their completed activities with the rest of the class.

Ideas for Children
Who Are Mechanically
Bright

Chapter Seven

I t is surprising that we place so much emphasis on verbal intelligence and verbal skills when we consider how mechanized our civilization has become. Our engineers receive honor and respect, but there is too little recognition given to the people whose mechanical skills keep our machines (and our lives) going smoothly.

Children with mechanical skills must be encouraged to use them and develop them further. They need to practice working with their hands, using tools, following plans and creating their own plans, seeing how things work, fixing broken things, and constructing new things.

It would also be good for all of the other pupils to learn some mechanical proficiency. Too many adults are unable to cope with the simplest machines in their environment, mainly because of having no experience with them.

This chapter gives some clues for identifying children who are mechanically bright. It tells how you can meet the needs of these pupils by having a class workshop. Complete plans (with instructions and diagrams) are given for the construction of a simple birdhouse for wrens. You will read how to challenge the mechanically gifted by bringing in and visiting resource people who will teach and stimulate pupils to learn more. It tells how to build an answer machine, which could be a stimulus to mechanical creativity. Suggestions will also be given for enjoyable and challenging activities to be used at meetings of a special club for the mechanically able students.

Who Are They?

Children who are mechanically bright can also be high in general intelligence. They show unusual ingenuity and enjoyment in solving mechanical problems.

The available tests on mechanical aptitude will screen out those with no aptitude — but they do not necessarily identify the mechanically gifted.

Since many children like to take things apart, this may not indicate giftedness in mechanics. However, interest would be one clue. The mechanically bright child cannot keep his hands off machines or gadgets. If he is not taking them apart to see how they work, he is touching them, looking intently at each part, and making them move.

The mechanically bright child is a joy to have around, because no matter what goes wrong, he can usually fix it. He knows how to adjust overhead projectors, microscopes, and filmstrip projectors. He can open stubborn drawers, open jars and bottles, and put film on a projector. What he doesn't know how to do, he can easily learn. He shows a confidence that things will work, and he doesn't panic the way most people do. Try to have at least one student like this in your class, if you can possibly arrange it, because they're practically indispensable.

All the King's Horses and All the King's Men — Enjoying a Class Workshop

Plan ahead for a class workshop by collecting old and broken mechanical clocks, radios, toasters, and can openers. To take these apart, the children would need screwdrivers, pliers, and various sizes of wrenches.

To practice the basic skills of using tools, you could get an assortment of screws, bolts, nuts, hammers, nails, a vise, and wood. To start with, a child could try to hammer a nail into a piece of soft wood, as it takes practice to get the nail in straight. Next, he could try putting a wood screw into the piece of wood, using a screwdriver. He could try fitting together various sizes of nuts and bolts. This is basic mechanics; and these skills will be needed by every adult, not just men.

It's interesting that the thing most children like to take apart is clocks, the bigger the better. From clocks they can learn more about the actions of gears than any other way. Your work table should have at least one discarded mechanical alarm clock.

1. Remove the cover from the clock with a screwdriver and a pair of pliers.

2. Look for the spring which turns the gears.

3. Try to figure out which gears turn first.

4. Which gears turn the hour hand and the minute hand?

5. Use your tools to remove some of the gears. Use a hammer to knock the pins from the center of the gears, if necessary.

6. Count the number of teeth on a small gear and the number of teeth on a large gear.

7. Place the gears on a piece of wood, so that a large one turns a small one and then another large one. Use small nails to serve as pins.

8. Compare the speeds of the two gears.

The children will probably be able to take these things apart and see how they operate, but it is doubtful that they could put them back together again. The important thing is to see how these machines work and how the parts interact.

Tinkertoys[1] are great mechanical toys. They show and develop mechanical ability. If you have these sets or any parts of the sets, they can be useful.

Kindergarten children will enjoy construction play with

---

[1] "Tinkertoy," Questor Education Products, 1055 Bronx River Ave., Bronx, N.Y., 10472.

Bolt-Tight ™ /"Bolt Blocks,"[2] a set of 16 blocks, screws, a screwdriver, wood, metal, and a 2-inch diameter wheel.

An entirely new concept in construction toys called "fischertechnik"[3] will be very challenging for mechanically gifted children.

It consists of building blocks that interlock simply. Each block can be fastened to, on all six sides. There are no rectangular construction limitations. The high-precision parts can be used to build an unlimited variety of models. These models can be motorized or made more sophisticated by use of extra accessories. The accessories are the Electric Motor Pack and the Reduction Gear Pack. Every possible mechanical part needed for building is included or available.

The directions are very short and simple, and tell how to fit one block into another. There is one method which calls for the use of a black square tab for snug interlocking of blocks. Another method calls for the use of a round red tab for adjustable fastening, whereby one block can be rotated to allow construction at any angle. All moving parts, such as tires, pulleys, gears, and cams, are fastened to axles with the red hubs. Children loosen hub, insert gear or tire, and tighten hub. Axles can be fitted through any of the four or five slots of the building blocks. Tires can be used as gears or pulleys.

A catalogue shows detailed pictures of many things that can be constructed. This set will encourage the mechanically able child to use his own ideas and experiment in building new things.

Machine Tools[4] is a book that will interest mechanically gifted children. It describes and pictures the common parts of important machine tools. It also tells what machinists and specially gifted machinists do in their work.

Once your pupils are able to work with tools, they will be eager to build something. Begin with something simple, so that they will experience success.

The complete plans and directions are given here for the construction of a birdhouse for wrens. The pattern given is one of

---

[2] Bolt-Tight ™ / "Bolt Blocks," T740/CO521, $4.95. Creative Playthings, Princeton, New Jersey 08540.

[3] "Fischertechnik," Fischer of America, Inc.; 1317 Broad St., Clinton, N.J. 07018. Creative Playthings, Princeton, N.J. 08540.

[4] Herbert S. Zim and James R. Skelly, *Machine Tools* (New York: William Morrow & Company, 1969).

Craft Patterns No. 308, "Wren Gable,"[5] from the *Junior Jig-Saw Packet.*

GABLE

Figure 7-1

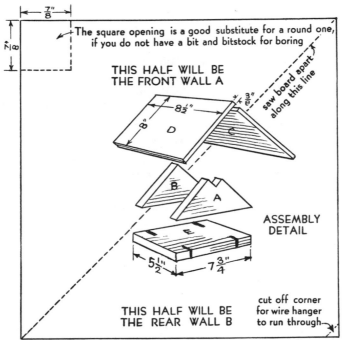

FULL-SIZE PATTERN FOR ENDS A & B
WREN GABLE

Figure 7-2

---

[5] "Three Wren Houses," Craft Patterns, No. 308, *Junior Jig-Saw Packet,* A. Neely Hall Productions, Elmhurst, Illinois.

HOW TO MAKE THE
WREN GABLE

The Wren Gable is about as simple a house as you can build. It requires only five pieces of wood. Front and rear walls A and B can be cut from a box board 3/4" thick. It is easy to lay them out. First, cut a board 5½" square. Then draw a diagonal line from one corner to an opposite corner, as indicated by dotted line. Cut away one corner of front wall for a doorway. The square opening is just as good as a round one, and it is easier to make, especially if you do not own a 7/8" bit for boring. Roof boards C and D need be only 3/8" thick. Roof board C is 3/8" narrower than board D to allow for the overlapping edge. Nail the roof boards to the end walls, with projections equal. Bottom board E may be cut from a box end board. Make it 5½" wide and 7¾" long, or to fit the house exactly. Slot the front and back edges of the bottom board as shown, with a saw. Fasten the board to the end walls with four screw-hooks. Screw the hooks into the lower edge of end walls A and B in the right positions to fit in the slots of bottom E. To hold the bottom board in place, turn the hook ends a quarter turn after slipping it over them. Use finishing-nails 1" and 1¼" long for assembling.

When the Wren Gable has been put together, sandpaper its surfaces smooth and give them two coats of white, green, or brown outdoor paint. Then get a piece of heavy wire and loop it through peak openings, for the hanger.

A book that you will find very valuable for children who like to work with their hands is *Building with Balsa Wood.*[6] This liberally illustrated book practically guarantees success in construction with this soft wood. It shows you how you don't need a lot of complicated, expensive equipment to work with balsa wood. You'll need a single-edged razor blade, an Exacto knife with a

[6] John Lidstone, *Building with Balsa Wood* (New York: Van Nostrand Reinhold Co., 1965).

heavier blade, scissors, paintbrush, a few pins, and quick-drying glue. The book shows you how to cut, pin, glue, sand, saw, carve, measure, true up, and bend the wood. You'll find that one of the best qualities of balsa wood is its ability to bend into many shapes. The book also shows you how to use model airplane glue to fasten tissue or cellophane to parts of your projects.

An informative book called *Machines* will be useful for all elementary students who wish to go beyond the basic knowledge of the simple machines.[7] The material is presented in a clear, interesting way.

Third graders and older students will enjoy and learn from *Simple Machines and How We Use Them.*[8] The book tells about all of the simple machines and their uses, and it has amusing, informative illustrations.

The First Book of Machines, for upper elementary students, tells the story of modern machines and how they do the world's work.[9] The book starts with the story of the first machines, goes on to modern machines, and relates how power is. applied to machines. Last of all, if tells about electric computers.

A fascinating book for upper elementary students, *The Wonders of Robots,* describes the robots that are all around us.[10] Unlike the tin woodman in *The Wizard of Oz,*[11] by Lyman Frank Baum, many of these robots are small, like the home thermostat. There is a good chapter on "Robots in Space" and one that tells about digital computers — robot brains.

The World of Push and Pull[12] will help third graders and older students understand the laws of mechanics, and thereby learn why things happen as they do. The clearly written text and interesting photographs give children a good start in understanding the rules that govern the motions of the universe.

---

[7] Irving and Ruth Adler, *Machines,* The "Reason Why" Books (New York: The John Day Company, 1965).

[8] Tillie S. Pine and Joseph Levine, *Simple Machines and How We Use Them* (New York: McGraw-Hill Book Company, 1965).

[9] Walter Buehr, *The First Book of Machines* (New York: Franklin Watts, Inc., 1962).

[10] Michael Chester and William Nephew, *The Wonders of Robots,* The Wonders of Science Library, (New York: G.P. Putnam's Sons, 1962).

[11] Lyman Frank Baum, *The Wizard of Oz* (New York: Macmillan Company, 1962).

[12] Earl Ubell, *The World of Push and Pull* (New York: Atheneum, 1964).

A book for bright third graders and much older students is *More Easy Physics Projects: Magnetism • Electricity • Sound.*[13] Each project is written up as an experiment, with the materials needed, the directions, and the concepts clearly given. Excellent drawings illustrate each project. This book should be very helpful for students doing independent work.

Upper elementary and junior high students will enjoy and learn from reading *Seesaws to Cosmic Rays: A First View of Physics.*[14] It discusses the sciences of mechanics, heat, electricity, light, and sound. The book also investigates radiation studies and the world of atomic structure, as well as the contributions that eminent scientists have made to physics. The color illustrations are excellent.

Advanced students will benefit from the book *Wonders of Gravity.*[15]

Your upper elementary mechanical whizzes will be delighted with the book, *What Makes TV Work?*[16] Its clear text and simple diagrams will help them understand a very complex subject, but tell your students not to expect to be able to fix their TV sets right away.

A very fine set of instructional materials that will be useful for intermediate through junior high school students is "The Work of Simple Machines."[17] The five color filmstrips acquaint students with the six basic simple machines, their mechanical advantages, and how to measure their work. Examples from everyday life demonstrate the six different types of machines in use. Accompanying recordings are presented in separate segments to facilitate the "single concept" method of teaching. Special frames at the beginning of each filmstrip introduce new vocabulary terms. There are three records (or cassettes) and five teacher's guides.

---

[13] Rocco V. Feravolo, *More Easy Physics Projects: Magnetism•Electricity•Sound* (Englewood Cliffs, N.J.: Prentice-Hall, Inc., 1968).

[14] Mitchell Wilson, *Seesaws to Cosmic Rays: A First View of Physics* (New York: Lothrop, Lee & Shepard Co., Inc., 1967).

[15] Rocco V. Feravolo, *Wonders of Gravity* (New York: Dodd, Mead & Co., 1965).

[16] Scott Corbett, *What Makes TV Work?* (Boston: Little, Brown and Company, 1965).

[17] Edward Victor, Ed. D., Professor of Science Education, Northwestern University, Consultant; "The Work of Simple Machines," 405-SR — set of 5 filmstrips, 3 records, and 5 teacher's guides; 405-STC — set of 5 filmstrips, 3 cassettes, and 5 teacher's guides; Society for Visual Education, Inc., 1345 Diversey Parkway, Chicago, Ill. 60614.

Children with mechanical interests will benefit from the filmstrip "Finding Out About Electricity," first in a series on basic intermediate science.[18] It is suggested for average fourth and fifth grade use. The filmstrip introduces new words at the start and asks questions. It goes on to tell about dry cells and solar batteries. Its diagram shows students how to make a simple generator by assembling a compass, magnet, and wire coil. They move the magnet through the coil and the electric current will move the compass needle. The filmstrip also discusses conductors, non-conductors, circuits, short circuits, and switches.

Another excellent teaching aid that you will find useful is "Machines — the Energy Savers," a tape and teacher's manual.[19] It has suggestions for drawings to be made on the board, questions, vocabulary, experiments, and "One Step Beyond" for enrichment. "The Wheel and Modern Man" is also interesting.

It is suggested that you use many, many audiovisual materials and as much actual shop and building practice as you can in this field. Allow plenty of time for playing around with the materials, for looking at them, and for trying out different approaches to problems. You will find that your books will be most useful after some actual manipulation of materials and after seeing many filmstrips and pictures.

Guest Stars

Invite as many mechanical experts in (as resource people) as possible. Try to get carpenters, mechanics, plumbers, electricians, racing car drivers or mechanics, and anyone else who works with machines. It will be very difficult to get these busy people to give up their time to come to school. However, if you have any parents of pupils who work in these fields, you have a very good chance of arranging a visit. If this is not feasible, you may be able to get these experts to allow an on-the-job visit by your students. Respect the experts' wishes about the number of children they can invite, as it takes a great deal of space (and patience) to handle an entire class. You may have to select a specified number of pupils for the visit, basing your choices on those who have demonstrated

---

[18] Lawrence F. Hubbell, Ph. D., Science Consultant, Oak Park Schools, Oak Park, Ill.; "Finding Out About Electricity," A 434-1, MCMLXIII, Society for Visual Education, Inc.

[19] "Machines — the Energy Savers," SG-515; "The Wheel and Modern Man," SG-54; Discovering Through Science, 1966; Imperial International Learning Corporation, Kankakee, Illinois.

great interest in mechanical subjects and those who have an aptitude for mechanics.

If you cannot arrange for your own resource people, be sure to sign up early in the school year with your local Volunteer Bureau (if you are fortunate enough to have one). It's amazing how many talented people they can find who are willing to come in to speak and demonstrate things for your pupils.

Never forget your "mechanic in residence" — your school engineer or custodian. He may be willing to take small groups of students downstairs to the boiler room to show them how the boilers work, and to demonstrate his work with them, if you plan ahead with him. He can also show them the duct work that carries the steam. He is a valuable resource person for any tool you forgot how to use, or any machine that "refuses to cooperate."

Arrange at least one field trip to a service station for a few interested students (after school, if necessary). It would be impossible to fit a whole class into a service station's mechanic's shop. This trip will probably be the high point of your school year if you plan it ahead. Be sure to find a cooperative service station owner, and find out when he is the least busy. A good (and helpful) mechanic can lift the hood of a car, raise a car up on a lift, and open a new mechanical world for your students. You will all leave the mechanic's shop with increased knowledge and tremendous respect for these talented people.

Building an Answer Machine

Read aloud part of the book, *Danny Dunn and the Homework Machine.*[20] Read chapters 4 and 5, "Meet Miniac" and "The Homework Machine Is Born." Get a good discussion going about building an answer machine.

Try to stimulate the mechanically gifted children in your group to create ideas for their own answer machine that they could build together. They may be able to work out simple electric circuits to give *yes* or *no* answers when the circuits are completed. Only low-voltage batteries should be used. If children are not successful in figuring out the circuits, this is your

---

[20] Jay Williams and Raymond Abrashkin, *Danny Dunn and the Homework Machine* (New York: McGraw-Hill Book Company, 1958), pp. 33-50.

opportunity to teach the concepts. They can then build many interesting things based on circuitry.

Students may design roll-up devices on the centers of two bathroom tissue rolls, with the answers on one roll and the questions on the other. These rolls would be hidden in a box, and the questions and answers would be seen through properly spaced openings in the box. Let children figure out how to design the machine for turning and matching.

If students need help or suggestions with an answer machine, the following device can accommodate a large number of multiple-choice questions and answers if it has a large diameter.

The machine consists of two cardboard discs attached at the center with a brass fastener. The radius of the top disc should be approximately ½ inch smaller than the bottom disc. Put the numerals of the questions on the visible outside edge of the bottom disc. The answer letters will be written on a hidden part of the bottom disc. When an arrow on the top disc points to a question numeral on the bottom disc, the answer will automatically appear through an opening in the top disc. Children can cut the opening in the top disc, turn the arrow to each question numeral, and write each answer letter in the opening.

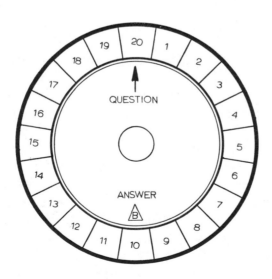

Figure 7-3

Now that you have your answer machine, you need multiple-choice questions and answers. Divide the class into small groups to write questions with multiple-choice answers. Select verbally gifted children to lead each group. Students can make up the questions. However, they will have to look up the correct answers. The pupils will need some stimuli to help them write good questions. Write a few subject headings on the blackboard, and discuss some possible items under each to get the children started. Remind students of some units they can review. Skimming textbooks and encyclopedias can give them ideas too. Have children write four alternative answers for each question, lettering each answer.

When you're ready to match the questions and answers to the machine, number each question, and change your multiple-choice alternatives so that the correct answer corresponds to the answer given on the machine.

The answer machine can be useful for marking daily papers and for tests, if you have enough questions.

The Live Wires Club

Plan a special club for your students who are mechanically bright and for those who are interested in the subject of mechanics.

Be on hand at all meetings to give suggestions and help, and for safety reasons. If you have not already done so for the entire class, try to have at least one session at the start that gives tips on the safe use of tools and electrical equipment.

You will have a great variety of activities for your club members to choose from. These will range from building things and taking things apart to physics experiments, electrical tinkering and construction, and craft work. Since intelligence is basic to talent in mechanics, these gifted children are usually above average, and they will do well in crafts requiring construction and manipulation. They will also be able to build and understand simple machines and their many uses.

Children can make imaginative paper constructions with simple materials. Use a very fine book called *Paper Construction for Children.* [21] Have youngsters try to make a ferris wheel and a merry-go-round.

The simple directions for constructing a "Sky Ride" are given below. They are reproduced from this book with the publisher's permission.

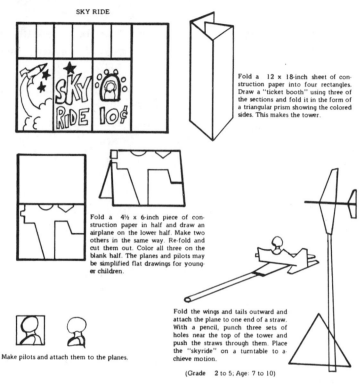

SKY RIDE

Fold a 12 x 18-inch sheet of construction paper into four rectangles. Draw a "ticket booth" using three of the sections and fold it in the form of a triangular prism showing the colored sides. This makes the tower.

Fold a 4½ x 6-inch piece of construction paper in half and draw an airplane on the lower half. Make two others in the same way. Re-fold and cut them out. Color all three on the blank half. The planes and pilots may be simplified flat drawings for younger children.

Make pilots and attach them to the planes.

Fold the wings and tails outward and attach the plane to one end of a straw. With a pencil, punch three sets of holes near the top of the tower and push the straws through them. Place the "skyride" on a turntable to achieve motion.

(Grade 2 to 5; Age: 7 to 10)

Figure 7-4

Your students will enjoy making some of the things demonstrated in the book *Building with Cardboard.* [22] A miniature stage built from a cardboard box would be an excellent project. It could be used for puppet productions. This book teaches how to make sculpture, space designs, a plane, and many other models. The photographs show every step in detail.

[21] Norman Krinsky and Bill Berry, *Paper Construction for Children* (New York: Van Nostrand Reinhold Company© 1966), p. 44.

[22] John Lidstone, *Building with Cardboard* (Princeton, N.J.: D. Van Nostrand Company, Inc., 1968).

Corrugated wrapping paper can be used to build a surprising variety of constructions, including a spiral runway, a merry-go-round, a wheel and axle, a scaffold, a pyramid, animals, people, and gears. A most unusual book with very good photographs, *Creating with Corrugated Paper*, can provide directions and inspiration.[23]

The Gadget Book will be one of your best resources for children with mechanical ability.[24] In a very interesting way, it shows how to make lighthouses, weather vanes, a magnet game, monorail systems, a spool cannon, a hand-held sail, a simple flashlight, a burglar alarm, and useless gadgets. The book gives only the basic principles of how and why the gadgets work, with good illustrations. Tricky or critical parts are discussed in detail. But a lot of the materials, sizes, and ways of assembling parts are left up to the child, so that he will use his imagination and ingenuity, and be able to take pride in his gadget as his own.

Your bright third grade club members may wish to try some experiments[25] that deal with mechanics as well as science:

Problem: How does an airplane fly?
Ask the question. Discuss flight of a bird. Wings push backward against air and send bird forward (thrust). Ask how children think an airplane flies using this principle. Ask: What is the job of the propellers? How can you increase thrust?

Materials:

toy airplane with rubber-band motor running its propellers.

Procedure:

1. Wind rubber band fully to spin propeller fast. Measure thrust.
2. Wind propeller halfway and try again.

Understandings:

Propellers are used to compress air and push it

---

[23] Rolf Hartung, *Creating with Corrugated Paper* (New York: Reinhold Publishing Corporation, 1966).

[24] Harvey Weiss, *The Gadget Book* (New York: Thomas Y. Crowell Company, 1971).

[25] "Mechanics — Force and Motion," Science Curriculum, Grade Three, 1966. The Wilmette Public Schools, District #39, Wilmette, Illinois.

backward. This gives thrust. Increased thrust leads to an increase in speed.

For extra work, children can find out information about man's attempt to fly. Include da Vinci, Montgolfier, and the Wrights.

Discuss rockets used in uplifting satellites. Explain that the next experiment will show how they exert a downward push in order to move upwards:

Objectives: Students can:

    1. Follow the directions of the experiment.
    2. Answer questions about action-reaction.

Materials: a long balloon
    a rubber band
    a plastic toy car about 8 inches long
    a paper clip

Procedure: 1. Inflate the balloon and secure opening with a paper clip so that air does not escape.
    2. With a rubber band, attach balloon to top of a toy car, with the opening of balloon toward rear of car.
    3. Place the car on the floor and release paper clip from the balloon. Observe.
    4. Ask these questions:
      a. In which direction does the auto move? (forward)
      b. In which direction does the air from the balloon move? (backward)
    5. Encourage pupils to do research to find out:
      a. How man uses action-reaction to make vehicles move.
      b. How a sailboat and a car move in one direction by exerting a force in an opposite direction.
      c. About the flight of a bird — how its wings push backward against air and send the bird forward.
      d. How an airplane flies using this principle.
      e. What is the job of the propellers?

The color film "Making Things Move" introduces the concepts of force and motion, and will be interesting for children who have done these experiments.[26]

Your group may wish to try an experiment with two inclined planes with different angles. Roll a roller skate down each one. Time what happens in each case with a stopwatch. Is there a difference in the amount of time it takes for the skate to reach the floor? Which inclined plane takes longer?

CHECKLIST

Mechanically bright children show their talent by their constant interest and skill in looking at and working with machines and gadgets.

Plan ahead for a class workshop where tools, wood, and assorted mechanical objects are available to use, take apart, and look at.

Have at *least* one old mechanical clock on your work table.

Collect and have available appropriate construction toys.

Give instruction and have many books on hand to teach the safe use of tools.

Allow some pupils to build a simple project, following detailed plans.

Have ready many, many audiovisual aids that teach the uses of simple machines, the laws of mechanics, and electricity.

Provide a rich assortment of books that demonstrate, explain, and add to students' knowledge after they have had actual experiences, and following the use of other audiovisual aids.

Invite or visit mechanical experts of all kinds.

Plan at least one field trip to a service station's mechanic's shop for a few interested students.

Try to stimulate mechanical creativity by having some students build an answer machine, providing as little help as possible.

Organize a special club where the mechanically able and interested students can build, experiment, or just putter together.

Help the club plan a wide variety of experiences that range from taking things apart to craft work.

---

[26] "Making Things Move," 11 minutes, color, No. 2013, Primary, Encyclopaedia Britannica Educational Corp. Film Library, 1822 Pickwick Ave., Glenview, Illinois 60025.

Ideas for Those Who Are Mathematically Bright

Chapter Eight

W e live in a world of numbers, most of which are too large for us to comprehend. Never before has mankind needed mathematical skills as much, since most of our scientific and engineering advances are based on them. We must treasure and nurture all talent in mathematics. Society cannot afford to waste it because a student is bored and understimulated. Too many potential mathematicians and scientists get sidetracked into fields that do not make full use of these rare talents. The logic and beauty of pure mathematics can be understood and *appreciated* by more of our students if we challenge them and keep them involved.

In this chapter, you will learn a few ways to identify the mathematically bright, and you will find many suggestions for their instruction. There are sections on setting up and using a class store, how to play "Factor Hopscotch," studying probability, graphing preferences, and planning a class company. Ideas are also given on how to conduct a special club for students with mathematical talent and great interest in mathematics.

How to Identify Them

There are some clues to mathematical giftedness when a child is very young — an interest in numbers, clocks, and calendars. A talented child has exceptional mathematical reasoning, an unusually good memory, and persistence in working toward a goal. He is way ahead of his classmates in mathematical accomplishments. He loves to measure everything. This kind of gift shows up in high scores on the mathematical parts of IQ tests and standardized achievement tests, and is usually found in pupils who are above 120 in IQ.

There are kinds of brightness that are commonly found together, like talent in science and mathematics. Watch extra closely those of your students who are gifted in science. They may also be bright in mathematics. Let us hope so, for their sakes, as they are going to need it.

Suggestions for Instruction

Emphasize more of the pure or abstract mathematics with gifted children, if you can. Avoid much memorization and extensive practice with them. They love to think through difficult problems and puzzles.

Have these children find simple geometric figures that are hidden in complex forms or patterns.

*   *   *   *   *   *   *   *

Talented pupils will learn by making up problems, using data presented in a paragraph containing many numerical statements. The paragraph could give the price of a house with its down payment, and the interest rate on the mortgage. You could include heating charges, time payments on a new stove and refrigerator, added insulation installed because it would reduce heating costs by a certain per cent, and many other facts. Pupils could figure out a variety of problems based on expenses related to this house.

There is no limit to the complexity of the problems and the

creativity needed to compose them if you have enough interesting data.

Students are to compose the problems, write their answers, and check their work. They will also enjoy solving each other's problems.

*　*　*　*　*　*　*　*

A study of Einstein and how he formulated the equation E = mc² will be stimulating. Gifted students will be fascinated by the history of mathematical ideas.

Children who are talented in mathematics will enjoy evaluating some of the quantitative reasoning they find in newspapers. They will like to make up their own problems using data found in the news media, and they can experiment with different ways of solving these problems.

"Stock Market"

Upper elementary and junior high students will be interested in a "Stock Market" game played with the newspaper. Each student will pretend to invest $100 in different stocks of his choice. Some may choose stocks that relate to their parents' jobs. They will watch the prices of their stocks each day and chart them on a graph for a set period of time.

When the set time period is up, students will figure their profits or losses. You may wish to continue this activity by having students figure their per cent of profit or loss, based on their original investments.

The personal involvement over a period of time of stock watching can make this project a great deal of fun. It is also an opportunity for interested students to learn more about our stock market.

*　*　*　*　*　*　*　*

The following unit can be used successfully to challenge upper elementary and junior high school students.

Bill's Party

Bill was planning a party for his friends, and he wanted to do nearly everything himself. Part of Bill's menu is given below. He had a little trouble figuring out some of his measurements. Will you help him?

Sour Cream Onion Dip (with Chips)

Ingredients:

3 - 12 ozs. cartons of sour cream
2 - packages of onion soup mix

Bill was having a great time mixing the sour cream with the onion soup mix, once he figured out how much sour cream to add.

The recipe calls for one package of onion soup mix for every pint of sour cream. The sour cream he bought did not come in pints. Bill wanted to make as much dip mix as possible using the above ingredients.

Problem:

If Bill used both of the packages of the onion soup mix, how much sour cream did he have left?

Answer:

The 3 cartons of sour cream equalled 36 ozs. Bill needed 32 ozs. The 36 ozs. minus the 32 ozs. left 4 ozs. of sour cream.

* * * * * * * *

Next Bill made some hot appetizers which he called "Puppies in a Blanket." They were fun to do, except that he couldn't come out even with his biscuits and his small frankfurters. He needed 60 appetizers.

Puppies in a Blanket

Ingredients:

3 packages of ready-to-bake biscuits (10 biscuits to a package)
3 packages of small frankfurters (24 frankfurters to a package)

Bill began by cutting each biscuit in half and wrapping each half around one frankfurter. When he finished one package of biscuits, he decided to cut each biscuit in three parts from then on. It was fun to cut the biscuits and wrap them around the small frankfurters. He placed them in a greased pan. Bill baked the wrapped frankfurters in a preheated 425° oven for about 12 minutes.

Problems:

What did Bill have left over?

How many?

Answers:

He had 6-2/3 biscuits and 12 small frankfurters left over.

* * * * * * * *

During a free period for independent mathematics work in a primary classroom, some children were working on these questions:[1]

1. What is the size of each tile in the floor of this room?

2. How many tiles are there in this room?

Two boys were very busy measuring the floor tiles. When it came to answering the second question, one child started counting all of the tiles in the room. The other, a very bright child in many ways, came up to his teacher and asked, "Gee, do I have to count *all* of those tiles?"

His teacher answered, "I don't know. What do you think?"

The boy wrinkled up his brow, worried for a while, and then asked, "Couldn't I just count them down and then across, and multiply the two numbers?"

This type of thinking can come from having the opportunity to measure real things, and from a teacher's provocative questions.

* * * * * * * *

---

[1] Peggy Pressley, Middlefork School, Sunset Ridge School District #29, Northfield, Illinois.

A child of this type will especially benefit from a three-level program of activities called *Measure and Find Out,* which can be used as supplementary work in science and mathematics.[2] The three consumable lab workbooks invite each student to use the tools, make the measurements, and record the data. The student works alone or in small groups.

A valuable resource for mathematics instruction is the magazine *The Arithmetic Teacher.* It will provide good ideas for all students, but especially fine activities for your pupils who are bright in mathematics.

One useful article in this magazine stresses the importance of exploration and free experiment with a new concept before the pupils are questioned and expected to discuss their findings.[3] This very sound method will usually save teaching time in the long run. It, of course, need not be confined to mathematics. It is also necessary in scientific inquiry and other learning.

The author gives many suggestions. The article illustrates discovery learning that began with the measurement of a rock — its perimeter and its thickness. It goes on to show how the children discovered the real meaning of volume by placing a rock in a container of water and measuring the displacement of the water when the rock was put in the container. The author also provides sound advice on using the activity of measuring well, giving it a purpose and a problem.

Since drill is the type of work that bright pupils hate, necessary practice can be made challenging by using *Cross-Number Puzzles,* self-checking puzzles that are worked just like crossword puzzles.[4] They are packaged in a lab for whole numbers that ranges from a grade three to grade six level. There is one consumable Student Record Book for each child, containing the blank cross-number puzzle forms. There are puzzles that practice addition, subtraction, multiplication, and division. There are also

---

[2] Clifford E. Swartz, Professor of Physics, State University of New York at Stony Brook, *Measure and Find Out* (Glenview, Illinois: Scott, Foresman and Company, 1969).

[3] Edith E. Biggs, "What's *your* position on the role of experience in the learning of mathematics?" *The Arithmetic Teacher,* May, 1971, Volume 18, Number 5, pp. 278-95.

[4] Mark Murfin, Ed. D., and Jack Bazelon, *Cross-Number Puzzles,* Science Research Associates, Inc., 259 E. Erie St., Chicago, Ill. 60611, 1966.

mixed practice and bonus puzzles. The problems are on separate cards, marked with different symbols to denote the kind of problem.

A subtraction puzzle card could have problems like these:

la

across

1	67 - 5
3	29 - 7
4	77 - 5
6	38 - 4

down

1	69 - 7
2	35 - 4
4	77 - 3
5	29 - 6

Each time a student completes one kind of computation, he may take home a bonus puzzle in that category. This informs the child's parents about the skills he is practicing.

The *Cyclo•teacher Learning Aid* can be used effectively for independent study in other subjects, but it is an exceptionally good device to stimulate and challenge the child who is bright in. mathematics.[5] This learning aid consists of a round teaching machine into which the pupil inserts special lessons, or Cycles, and sheets of blank paper for his written answers.

The child uses the Index in the file of Cycle lessons to choose a Cycle that meets his needs and interests. He reads the instructions in the center of the first side of the Cycle to make sure he has the knowledge and skills to work the Cycle. If not, he takes an easier Cycle. Key questions are identified on each Cycle, and if the pupil misses one, he should repeat the side until he can answer all the Key questions correctly. On the second side of each Cycle, the sections Related Cycles and Related Articles suggest extensions to strengthen the pupils' learning of that Cycle's material.

---

[5] *Cyclo•teacher Learning Aid,* Field Enterprises Educational Corp., Merchandise Mart Plaza, Chicago 54, Illinois.

A set of very challenging color filmstrips for able fifth graders that will keep them on their toes is called "The World of Whole Numbers."[6] Some of the titles are "The Doughnut Stand," "The Missing Addend," "Sporting Mathematics," "Bowler's Mathematics," and "The Missing Factor."

"The Doughnut Stand" is very good. There are simple problems like the following:

Glazed doughnuts cost 10¢ each.
How much will 4 chocolate-covered (at 8¢ each) and 3 glazed doughnuts cost?

$$4 \cdot 8 + 3 \cdot 10 = N¢$$
$$32 + 30 \quad\;\; = 62¢$$
$$N \quad\;\; = 62¢$$

There are many problems — some very complex.

I recommend that you allow plenty of time for the filmstrip. See to it that the student has paper, a pencil, and enough time so that he doesn't feel he just has to skim it. It's impossible to skim it and get anything out of it (except, perhaps, a taste for doughnuts).

A very fine kit to be used with Cuisenaire® Rods (the multi-colored wooden shapes for manipulative study of number) is called *Student Activity Cards for Cuisenaire® Rods*.[7] The kit consists of 66 cards in ten sets to be used with the rods. The cards are written for children's independent use and provide a wide variety of games, activities, and problems which develop mathematical concepts appropriate for grades K-six. Sets 1-4 are sequential and help to establish the relationships among the rods. Sets 6-9 are also sequential, as they develop more advanced concepts. The cards in Sets 5 and 10 can be used at any time.

Some good, easy books on mathematics for children through grade three are recommended below:

Straight Lines, Parallel Lines, Perpendicular Lines teaches the beginner to see lines around himself.[8]

---

[6] "The World of Whole Numbers" Nos. 35/324 — 35/327, Bailey-Film Associates, 2211 Michigan Ave., Santa Monica, Calif. 90404.

[7] Patricia Davidson, Arlene Fair, and Grace Galton, *Student Activity Cards for Cuisenaire® Rods;* Cuisenaire Company of America, Inc., New Rochelle, N.Y., 1971.

[8] Mannis Charosh, *Straight Lines, Parallel Lines, Perpendicular Lines* (New York: Thomas Y. Crowell Company, 1970).

In *Estimation,* making calculated guesses is clarified through various do-it-yourself projects.[9]

What Is Symmetry? is a book in which an alligator takes the reader through various examples of symmetry in nature and in man-made objects.[10]

A good book for students on the intermediate level is *Bosley on the Number Line.*[11] This is an adventure story with a mathematical plot, using sets, a number line, some characteristics of odd and even numbers, and the computing of addition, subtraction, and multiplication.

For pre-primary children, *GeoShapes* are math aids that have a game-like approach to basic concepts. [12] These domino-like tiles picturing circles, triangles, and squares are matched to each other or to a playing cube to help young children identify basic shapes in order to win games. A teacher's manual is included.

One third grade teacher puts the following numerals on the board with this provocative question: [13]

What can we do with these numbers?

7	8	56	6	7	42
6	8	48	7	9	63
8	9	72	7	4	28
9	4	36	8	4	32

Figure 8-1

In the class discussion about the question and numerals, she draws out the four multiplication and division facts that can be given for each group of numerals.

---

[9] Charles F. Linn, *Estimation* (New York: Thomas Y. Crowell Company, 1970).

[10] Mindel Sitomer and Harry Sitomer, *What Is Symmetry?* (New York: Thomas Y. Crowell Company, 1970).

[11] Alix Shulman, *Bosley on the Number Line* (New York: David McKay Co., Inc., 1970).

[12] E. Glenadine Gibb and Alberta M. Castaneda, *GeoShapes,* No. 02155; Scott, Foresman and Company, Glenview, Illinois.

[13] Audrey Werner, Middlefork School, Sunset Ridge School District #29, Northfield, Illinois.

The numerals can be changed each day, and later on, the processes can be mixed, with some groups making multiplication and division facts and others addition and subtraction facts.

A primary teacher has a unique way to stimulate pupils to do independent math work.[14] There is a Math Ladder made of masking tape on a wall near a counter top. The ladder has 50 rungs on it to show progress from one to 50. Each child in the class has a geometrical shape or combination of shapes to signify where he is on the ladder. Near the ladder on a counter are 50 folders, numbered one through 50, containing math work that is graded in difficulty, beginning with the simplest work sheets in folder one. The lower numbers contain some computation. The higher numbers have more story problems that children have to think about. Pupils are encouraged to do this independent work in their spare time and move up the Math Ladder.

Another primary teacher uses an idea for motivating children to master 100 multiplication facts by showing the following proclamation to the class early in the year:[15]

MATH PROCLAMATION

Hear Ye!   Hear Ye!
Know all Men
By This Declaration . . .
That: _____
Of   Room_____
                         Middlefork School
                         Northfield, Illinois

Has mastered the 100 multiplication facts
And: therefore is proclaimed proficient
In this school year of _____
By:

_____
                                        Teacher

When a pupil is ready to try for the 100 facts, he puts his

---

[14] Peggy Pressley, Middlefork School, Sunset Ridge School District #29, Northfield, Illinois.
[15] Margaret Goldman (and Sue Schwartz), Middlefork School, Sunset Ridge School District #29, Northfield, Illinois.

name on the board. Then the teacher tests him whenever she can. When pupils win the proclamations, they are posted on the bulletin board.

One third grade teacher plays the familiar game "Around the World" with mixed multiplication and division flash cards.[16] The teacher holds successive flash cards while a pupil acts as leader and goes around the class, standing behind each child in turn. When the teacher uncovers the flash card, the leader and the sitting child compete to give the correct answer. Ties are repeated. If the leader answers correctly first, he moves to the next sitting pupil. If the child who is sitting gives the correct answer first, the leader sits in his place, and the winner gets up and becomes the leader. To keep the game from getting too competitive, the teacher can help the leader compete with his *own* previous score of how far he got around the room. (This takes the emphasis off of competition between the leader and each individual he races against.)

Magic Squares

One elementary teacher uses magic squares for addition and subtraction.[17] A magic square is one in which each row, column, or diagonal has the same sum, in the case of addition.

The teacher assigns the sum and gives the student the blank squares. He is to fill in the numerals. For example:

21

6	11	4
5	7	9
10	3	8

45

12	27	6
9	15	21
24	3	18

Figure 8-2

Magic squares can be made into various sizes — 30 squares if desired, and any sum. Some can be used with only certain numerals.

---

[16] Audrey Werner, Middlefork School, Sunset Ridge School District #29, Northfield, Illinois.

[17] Joyce Arkin, Weber Elementary School, Parkway School District, Creve Coeur, Missouri.

Using a Class Store

Children in first grade can participate in a pretend store, using two flannel boards, so that all the pupils can observe what is happening. The buyer uses his flannel board as a purse, and the shopkeeper uses his as a cash register.[18] The book *Kindergarten-Primary Education; Teaching Procedures* also gives ideas on using a grocery store, so second graders can develop the concepts of *loaf, scale, peck, bushel,* and liquid measures.

Consumer Education — "Shopper"

The following game of "Shopper" can be used by bright third grade pupils. It is played with a pack of 36 cards, 27 of which have a problem for the player to solve. There are also nine surprise cards. The game can be extended for older pupils to provide practice in figuring out good buys when shopping.

This game can be played by three to eight players. One of the players acts as a cashier, and he does not receive cards. The winner of the game is the one with the most tokens when the game ends. It ends when all the cards in the pack are used up.

The cashier gives each player five cards and a pad of scratch paper. The player to the left of the cashier begins play by solving as many of his problem cards as he can, using the scratch pad of paper. He checks his answers with the cashier, who has an answer card, as he does each one. The cashier checks the answers given, and if the pupil answers correctly, the cashier gives him the stated number of tokens on his problem card.

You can have students help you make up this game for classroom use. They can compose their own problems, rule and cut the cards, and copy the text on each card, with the token value that is given for each.

The text for each of the 36 cards is given below:

A clerk sold 29 bags of candy. There were 6 pieces of candy in each bag. The clerk sold how many pieces of candy in all? (174) 2 TOKENS

Tim had some balloons. He bought 12 more balloons. Then

---

[18] Ida E. Morrison and Ida F. Perry, *Kindergarten-Primary Education; Teaching Procedures* (New York: The Ronald Press Company, 1961), pp. 478-79, 498-99.

he had 41 balloons in all. How many balloons did he have to begin with? (29 balloons) 4 TOKENS

Bob has to buy 72 cupcakes. Cupcakes are sold in packages of 4. How many packages will Bob have to buy? (18 packages) 5 TOKENS

Which container holds the most liquid — the one that holds 5 quarts or the one that holds 1 gallon? (5 quarts) 6 TOKENS

Carol bought 4 pints of milk. John bought 1 quart of milk. Who bought the most milk? (Carol) 7 TOKENS

A large gallon bottle holds the same amount of liquid as 8 pints. True or false? (true) 6 TOKENS

A clerk sold 8 quarts of milk. How many gallons did he sell? (2 gallons) 7 TOKENS

Jane needs 32 prizes for a party. Prizes are sold in boxes of 4. She will have to buy how many boxes of prizes? (8 boxes) 2 TOKENS

Steve spent $.39 for a whistle, $.59 for a toy clown, and $1.28 for a game. He spent how much money in all? ($2.26) 1 TOKEN

Karen needs 18 hats for a party. Party hats are sold in packages of 3. She will have to buy how many packages? (6 packages) 3 TOKENS

Mary spent 21¢ for toy dogs that cost 7¢ each. How many toy dogs did Mary buy? (3 toy dogs) 2 TOKENS

Mrs. Jones bought 88 paper cups for a party. Paper cups are sold in boxes of 8. How many boxes of paper cups did she buy? (11 boxes) 2 TOKENS

John spent 95¢ for some toys. He paid 5¢ for each toy. John bought how many toys? (19 toys) 7 TOKENS

Nancy bought 12 new paper dolls. Then she had 31 paper dolls in all. How many paper dolls did she have before she bought the 12? (19 paper dolls) 4 TOKENS

A clerk had 108 quarts of paint to sell. He sold 59 of the quarts. How many quarts of paint did he have left to sell? (49 quarts) 3 TOKENS

A yard of cloth is greater than 2 feet of cloth. True or false? (true) 4 TOKENS

7 feet of cloth are less than 2 yards of cloth. True or false? (false) 6 TOKENS

Is 3/4 of a yard more than 7/8 of a yard? (no)   8 TOKENS

Ted gave the cashier half of his money. John spent one-third of his money. Which boy spent the larger share of his money? (Ted)   6 TOKENS

Is 5/8 of a yard of cloth the same as 2/4 of a yard of cloth? (no)   5 TOKENS

Is 3/6 of a yard of cloth the same as 5/10 of a yard of cloth? (yes)   3 TOKENS

Ann bought some candy for $.16, and she gave the clerk a half dollar. How much change should she receive? ($.34)   4 TOKENS

Ellen spent 75¢ for toys. She then bought some candy for 29¢. She had a dollar with her. How much money does she still need? (4¢)   5 TOKENS

Jenny bought 17 inches of cloth. Bob bought 11 inches of cloth, and Jerry bought 7 inches of cloth. Did they buy more or less than a yard of cloth in all? (less)   8 TOKENS

Which is the bigger amount of cloth — 3 yards or 11 feet? (11 feet)   9 TOKENS

Two boys wanted to make sandwiches. One boy brought 1-1/2 loaves of bread. The other one brought 1-1/4 loaves. How much bread did they have in all? (2-3/4 loaves)   5 TOKENS

John's mother poured a can of soup that holds 10-1/2 ozs. into a pot. Then she added the same amount of water. She mixed them together and heated the soup. She divided the soup among her three children. How many ounces of soup did each child get? (7 ozs.)   9 TOKENS

COLLECT 5 TOKENS FROM THE CASHIER.
COLLECT 1 TOKEN FROM THE CASHIER.
PAY THE CASHIER 4 TOKENS.
PAY THE CASHIER 8 TOKENS.
COLLECT 7 TOKENS FROM THE CASHIER.
COLLECT 8 TOKENS FROM THE CASHIER.
COLLECT 4 TOKENS FROM THE CASHIER.
PAY THE CASHIER 1 TOKEN.
PAY THE CASHIER 3 TOKENS.

You can adapt this game for upper elementary students by giving them more challenging problems to solve. A few sample cards could be:

Which is the better buy? An 8 oz. can of tomato paste for 27¢ or a 12 oz. can of tomato paste for 36¢? (the 12 oz. can for 36¢)   5 TOKENS

Joe bought 2-1/2 lbs. of potatoes, 6-1/3 lbs. of onions, and 5-1/6 lbs. of meat. How much did they all weigh together? (14 lbs.)   6 TOKENS

STUFFO bread —   1 lb. size - 36¢
                              12 oz. size - 29¢
Which is the better buy? (1 lb. size)   6 TOKENS

YUMYUM chocolate bar — 8 oz. size - 25¢
                                     3 oz. size - 14¢
Which is the better buy? (8 oz. bar)   4 TOKENS

You may wish to use the game "Pay the Cashier."[19] This game teaches the following things:

the different coins and bills up to $10
the adding of bills and coins to make the amount of a purchase, just as a customer does in the store
the making of change in the store way, beginning with the amount of the purchase and counting up with coins or bills to the higher bill that is offered

One player is the Cashier, and the others are Customers. The spinner is used to choose the first Cashier and to tell which store is chosen. Each player begins with the same amount of money. Cards for each store give the player the kind and amount of his purchase. For example:

TOY STORE

Your parents gave you $2.50 to pick out your own present. But it costs you only $2.39.
Pay the Cashier . . .

The play continues until one player has no more money. Then the other players count their money and the winner is the one with the most money left.

---

[19] Edward W. Dolch, Ph.D., "Pay the Cashier" (Champaign, Illinois: Garrard Publishing Company, 1957).

Factor Hopscotch

Everyone will welcome an outdoor game for spring and fall. For cold or inclement weather, you may wish to play this in the gym, using chalk to draw the hopscotch game.

Factor Hopscotch is played just like the traditional game, with one exception. The numerals written in the boxes are products chosen by you to give multiplication practice and challenge.

There are many different versions of hopscotch. One form of it is given in Figure 8-3.

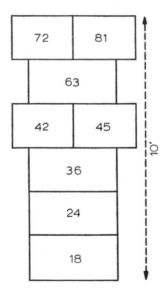

Figure 8-3

As many as four players can take part in this game. The first player throws a flat marker, or puck, to the first box. Before he is allowed to hop, he must give at least one multiplication combination for the product in the box. For example, if the product in the box is 24, any of the following answers would be accepted:

$$6 \times 4 \qquad 4 \times 6$$
$$8 \times 3 \qquad 3 \times 8$$
$$12 \times 2 \qquad 2 \times 12$$
$$24 \times 1 \qquad 1 \times 24$$

Combinations may not be repeated if there are others that can be given. One player acts as a checker and uses an answer sheet.

Change the products in the boxes for new games. This will introduce variety and provide extra stimulation.

If you wish to make the game progressively more difficult, first eliminate the factors that multiply by one. Then go on to ask for two multiplication combinations instead of one.

If the player gives the correct multiplication combination for the first box, he can begin at the starting line and hop over the first square into the second box. He then proceeds through boxes three, four, five, six, seven, and eight, placing both feet simultaneously in boxes four and five, and likewise in seven and eight.

When he has reached the far end of the playing space, his left foot should be in box seven and his right in box eight. He then jumps into the air and turns around, placing his left foot in eight and his right foot in seven; and he then returns to box two. When he reaches this square, he leans over and picks up his puck from the first square. He does this while standing on one foot and without touching the ground, except with the hand picking up the puck. He then hops into box one, and out of the playing field, being careful to hop completely over the starting line.

Next, he stands at the starting line and tosses his puck into square two. He continues in this same way until he cannot give correct factors, he misses the square with his puck, he steps on a line, or he loses his balance and puts both feet down (except in boxes four and five and seven and eight). Then it is the next player's turn.

The player who is first to return his puck to the starting line, after having given correct factors for each square, and after having placed the puck in each square in the order one, two, three, four, five, six, seven, eight, seven, six, five, four, three, two, one, is declared the winner.

You may wish to play one of the many other variations of the game, any of which will work out well with the multiplication factors.

Studying Probability

When you throw a penny in a probability experiment, there are two possible ways it can land. You can conduct a probability experiment with a die. When you toss a die, there are six possible ways it can land.

Try throwing a die 800 times. Take turns with someone in throwing the die and writing the result. As you throw the die, keep a tally sheet under the numerals one through six, counting by fives. When you get near the 800 throws, start counting closely. Add up your tallies. When you have finished, show the result on a special graph called a *histogram*.

Mathematicians claim that the more times you throw the die, the more probable it is you will throw each of the six numbers about the same number of times.

An experiment with throwing a die 800 times is recorded in Figure 8-4.

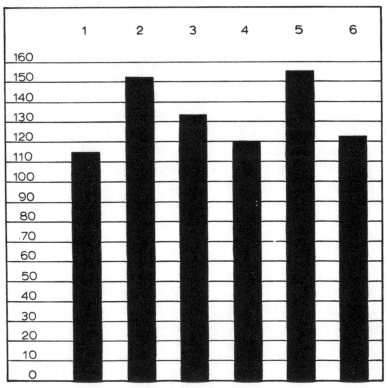

Figure 8-4

Extend your classroom walls by visiting exhibits of mathematical interest. For example, the Museum of Science and Industry in Chicago, Illinois has a special room devoted to mathematics.[20] They have a large exhibit on probability that is fascinating to watch.

Be sure to include study of the bell-shaped curve. It's interesting, especially to the mathematically talented child.

Graphing Preferences

An activity that has inherent interest for students is the graphing of their preferences. You can begin with their favorite sport, listing all of their suggested sports at the bottom of the graph, and the numerals on the left side. Go on to their favorite TV program, and then their favorite food, allowing students to select the subject graphed.

Planning a Class Company

For elementary students, the planning and operation of a class company can be a stimulating experience. Give your gifted students opportunities for challenge by selecting their responsibilities carefully. Your verbally gifted children will write advertising messages for the class, school, and P.T.A. publications. Give your socially bright pupils the chance to go out and sell your products or services, and an opportunity to lead a sales organization and organize people into a group effort. The artistic pupils can draw advertising posters, and the mathematically bright students will be responsible for keeping the records of expenses, sales, profits, and losses. They will be challenged by figuring prices for a real business.

There are many products and services that young pupils can provide so that your class can actively engage in a business. The actual product or service decided upon depends on the age of the students, your location, the time of the year, the availability of

---

[20] Museum of Science and Industry, E. 57th Street and Lake Shore Drive, Chicago, Illinois.

raw materials, the talents of your pupils, and the local demand for
these products or services.

Very young pupils in a warm climate, or in the late spring or
early fall in a cold climate, might go into the lemonade business.
They would shop for lemons and sugar, make the lemonade and
ice, and sell drinks by the glass at a profit. Children must maintain
strict standards of cleanliness. The stand could be open at
lunchtime, recess, and after school. The business might be
expanded to provide pupil-made cookies. Salesmen could cover
the neighborhood after school and on weekends with wagons full
of the lemonade and cookies. Exact records would be kept on
costs and sales, and profits would be divided among pupils.

Some suggested products are:

handmade embroidered aprons	plants in pots
appliquéd pot holders	painted cardboard napkin
decorated stationery	rings
birdhouses	candy
scrapbooks with decorated covers	

Some suggested services are:

lawn cutting	baby sitting
snow shoveling	leaf raking
weeding	dishwashing
dog walking	

Junior high and high school students can get into the
complexities of incorporation, studying the workings of a corporation as they sell stock and trade with it. Keep your class
corporation as simple as possible, but have students investigate all
the workings of a corporate business, including the issuing of
dividends.

High school classes will benefit from studying or joining in
the work of Junior Achievement.[21] You can write to them for
information or read about them.[22] Junior Achievement is a
nationwide, "learn-by-doing," practical economics program in
which high school students organize and manage their own

---

[21] Junior Achievement, 909 Third Avenue, New York, N.Y. 10022.
[22] Alfred Steinberg, "The Mini-Businesses of Junior Achievement,"
Reader's Digest, May, 1971, pp. 19-26. Reprinted and condensed from *The
Kiwanis Magazine*, April, 1971.

small-scale businesses under the guidance of adult advisers from business and industry.

Each Junior Achievement company is organized in the fall for one year as a corporate structure. There are approximately 20 students in each company. They are the board of directors, the working force, and the sales staff. They elect their own officers and they select a product to make or a service to render. They capitalize their business through public sale of capital stock at $1 a share. They set up production lines, plan distribution, and advertise, promote, and sell their company's product or service. Students pay themselves salaries and wages as management and the working force, and decide on sales commissions for themselves as salesmen. They keep company books and records. They pay rent for their work space and equipment, provided by the local organization, and they must meet depreciation charges on equipment and machinery. Students pay taxes, and they pay dividends to their stockholders if their enterprise is profitable. They liquidate their companies at the end of the program year and issue stockholder reports. Junior Achievers develop a realistic understanding of the organization and operation of a business enterprise.

The Unknown Factors — a Club

Your mathematically bright students will learn from and enjoy a special club. Any activity that makes them think, count, or measure something will be very challenging to them.

Try to provide problems like the following:

"Going in Circles"

A, B, C, and D start from the same point to walk around a circular piece of ground, whose circumference is 1 mile.

A walks 5 miles an hour, B 4 miles an hour, C 3 miles an hour, and D 2 miles an hour.

How long will it be before all four meet again at the starting point?

(Answer: 1 hour. By that time A will have gone around the circle five times, B 4 times, C 3 times, and D 2 times.)

The mathematically bright students will want to study

computers. Have them read everything available that is at their level. Arrange for opportunities for them to visit computers, if possible.

Another fascinating activity for club members is the study of the metric system. Students will enjoy finding the metric equivalents of things measured in feet and yards. They will look for opportunities to measure *everything*.

Investigate the many challenging learning materials for your club members. Get ideas from books and magazines to share with them.

Students can work independently with the teaching aid called "Mathematical Balance." [23] The balance has ten stations at each side on both front and back. Weights are placed on number pegs and show relationship between numbers, addition, subtraction, and multiplication. The reverse side of the arm is blank, and white self-adhesive labels are supplied so that each peg may be given fraction, money, length values, etc. Equations may also be solved on this balance. A teacher's guide and a set of 20 work cards are provided.

A delightful math book for young readers is *Weighing and Balancing.* [24] It shows the child how to make his own simple balance out of a piece of doweling rod, string, three cup hooks, and two stiff paper plates. There are suggestions of many unusual things to balance, for the purpose of comparing their weights. Balances made of metal coat hangers with metal clips, rods with paper cups, and others are illustrated very clearly. In this book the pupil learns a basic understanding of important principles of measurement, through do-it-yourself activities and experiments.

Some colorful materials for set work are the "Grouping and Setting Shapes" and "Grouping Circles." [25] These plastic materials can be used for individual or group work, and will be very helpful in teaching intersection of sets.

---

[23] L.G.W. Sealey, M. Ed. "Mathematical Balance," Nos. 95031, 95034, 95035. Invicta Plastics Limited. Dick Blick. P.O. Box 1267, Galesburg, Illinois 61401.

[24] Jane Jonas Srivastava, *Weighing and Balancing* (New York: Thomas Y. Crowell Company, 1970).

[25] "Grouping and Setting Shapes," "Grouping Circles," Nos. 95014, 95015. Invicta Plastics Limited. Dick Blick. P.O. Box 1267, Galesburg, Illinois 61401.

There are many other materials available for independent work in mathematics. Your club members will enjoy working on them as long as they provide opportunities to think.

CHECKLIST

Challenge students who are mathematically bright by making them think.

Some clues to mathematical giftedness: an early interest in numbers, clocks, calendars, and measurement; exceptional mathematical reasoning; an unusually good memory; persistence in working toward a goal; high math IQ scores; and high math achievement test scores.

Have students make up problems from data presented in a paragraph containing many numerical statements.

Interest pupils in the history of mathematical ideas.

Use the stock market reports in the newspaper to follow and graph selected stocks, charting and figuring profits or losses.

Have students figure solutions to problems from a unit about party plans.

Teach measurement by providing materials, time, and suggestions for real measurement experiences.

Use discovery learning by giving students opportunities to explore and experiment freely with new concepts before they are questioned or expected to discuss their findings.

Promote thinking by grouping related numerals, and ask pupils to tell what can be done with the numbers in each group.

Provide incentives for independent practice and for necessary memorization.

Play "Around the World" for variety in flash card practice.

Assign magic square sums, and have students fill in the squares.

Use a class store and shopping games to practice addition and subtraction skills, fractions, the use of money, and measurement facts.

Play "Factor Hopscotch" for multiplication practice and challenge.

Use the study of probability to interest bright students.

Provide graphing practice by graphing preferences in sports, foods, TV programs, etc.

Have students plan and operate a class company, increasing its complexity with the higher age levels.

Organize a special club for the mathematically bright, providing opportunities for independent and group study, provocative problems, the study of computers, and work with the metric system.

Using Games
to Stimulate Bright
Children

Chapter Nine

M any modern parents are frankly envious of their children's school life, with its many games and activities. Few of them worry that their youngsters are wasting time instead of learning, since most teachers use games well for the practice of skills.

Games that will be valuable for a bright child differ from those that provide special practice. They induce the child to plan, choose, solve problems, role-play, or get curious about some topic, place, or object.

Simulation games are particularly valuable for gifted children. These games require concentration and active participation. Short examples of this type of game are given, showing how they can motivate and lead bored pupils back into text materials and further learning.

Two sample games planned for bright pupils are provided for you. You may use them as they are, or you may want to employ the suggestions for adapting the games for your own level or age group.

Some basic elements of games are analyzed for you. You will

be shown how to create your own games for your particular needs. These games can be used to introduce or end units, and provide opportunities for thinking, as well as excitement.

One child complained to his teacher, "I not only know the answers, but I can even guess the questions before they come." If you have such a pupil, you can stimulate him to work up to his potential by using games as clues. Observe the child closely as he plays games in various subject areas. When he shows great interest or perseverance in a particular game, assign him a related topic for research and allow him to work independently while the class has regular lessons. Find other games on the subject that he can play by himself or with one other pupil. Bring him back into the daily lessons when you reach new work that he needs to learn. Using games to stimulate or discover interests will do more than excite the child and make him curious about new subjects. It will also prevent probable discipline problems and alienation that will eventually be caused by boredom.

What Makes a Game Fun?

A game is enjoyable because the player feels that he is playing instead of working. Games that accomplish this usually contain some elements of chance or surprise. It can be very exciting to plan a course of action, play a part, or solve a problem that has become your own.

The thrill of chance can be added to almost any game. A roll of the dice or the spin of a spinner can vary the number of moves you make on a board game, or the number of cards you draw in a card game. You can introduce variety into a game by adding wild cards or jokers to be used in place of any card you need. The fun of getting these wild cards and the varied ways you can use them make children want to play the game. Special direction cards add the element of luck by telling the player to move to various spaces on a board game, or to pay or receive play money or points.

The games that are most enjoyable are those in which the player can make progress or be turned back from a goal, win or lose points, or give up desired properties. All of this contributes to suspense and excitement. The child can compete in this type of game without having his ego threatened. He knows that he can lose without losing face.

Extremely gifted children may tire easily of games unless they are very complex. However, most very intelligent children enjoy thinking games of all kinds.

Use thinking games to stimulate creativity and more thought. Crossword puzzles, chess, Scrabble, and simulation games are examples of only a few.

Simulation Games

Simulations are motivational tools which attempt to select and simplify certain elements of real social situations. In these models of real life, the players act as decision-makers. They compete for objectives as they act as individuals or in teams to manage the affairs of nations, rulers, legislators, or consumers.

Simulation games are ideal for the bright student because they give him an opportunity to do critical thinking, solve problems, play the roles of different people, and make decisions, as well as learn concepts and processes. Many games are suitable for high school students and are very complex. However, some simpler simulations are available for fifth- and sixth-graders. It is very important to use these games for the level of pupil they were planned for.

A simulation game might have some of these elements:

> First, one must identify some objectives . . .[1]
> Second, the designer must construct a simplified model of the process or system that will best serve the objectives . . .
> Third, the various actors or teams must be identified, keeping in mind not only the number that would demonstrate the model effectively but also the classroom needs . . .
> Fourth, the actors must have resources (troops, money, votes, etc.) to exchange in competition with other players . . .
> Fifth, the actors as they engage in trading resources must have rather clear objectives or goals . . .
> Sixth, in any simulation there must be some

---

[1] Reprinted with permission from *Simulation Games for the Social Studies Classroom* published by Thomas Y. Crowell Company, New York. Copyright © 1968 by the Foreign Policy Association, pp. 14-15.

limits or rules set on what is permissible behavior. Also, time limits must be determined for the various stages of play, and procedures for exchanges must be spelled out . . .

Finally, some games begin with a "scenario" to set the stage and instruct the actors for the beginning of play . . .

The social studies are taught well by simulation games when the games are used with regular units of study. Simulations are still very new, and have not been tested long enough, but they can be used effectively to complement other materials and methods. They help students learn the importance of seeing someone else's point of view, and of good communication. This kind of game can teach students that their behavior can have real effects. Players will also discover that although they are playing a game, it requires real effort.

It is vital that a simulation game be followed up by in-depth discussion. In talking over the experiences of the game, players should be encouraged to relate them to events that have happened in the real world. Many misconceptions can be cleared up by this essential process. This is the teacher's opportunity to help the players discover that the game has simplified the world they live in, and that real crises are even more complex and difficult to deal with.

"Dangerous Parallel"[2]

"Dangerous Parallel," a simulation in international diplomacy, can motivate eighth through twelfth grade students into top level decision-makers. The teacher uses a record with a filmstrip that defines simulation, explains the playing, and gives a strategic briefing. She also has a Control Manual and a Consequences Calculator. Each team uses Badges, Easels, Decision-Choice Wheels, Crisis Manuals, Information Files, Top-Secret Resource Envelopes, Decision-Maker's Checksheets, and a Decision Report Pad.

[2] Scott, Foresman and Company, 1900 E. Lake Ave., Glenview, Illinois 60025. Developed by the Foreign Policy Association.

DANGEROUS PARALLEL models aspects of the international system at the time of the Korean War.[3] The simulation world includes six disguised nations, each of which is represented by four or five ministers: Chief Minister, Foreign Minister, Defense Minister, Political Minister, and Economic Minister (optional). These nations, as play begins, find themselves in the midst of a serious international crisis. They are provoked by an attack by one small nation upon its neighbor. One major power has already entered the conflict and is faced with the question of whether it should cross a boundary to pursue the enemy of its small ally. If it does, other major nations are then faced with the dilemma of whether they should intervene and, if so, with what consequences.

The student decision-makers must analyze the various military, political, economic, ideological, and psychological factors involved in their nation's course of action. After formulating their own objectives and seriously considering those of other nations, they must pursue their nation's best interests through diplomacy, negotiation, or armed force.

At the end of each round, the six nations have to choose from 24 alternative choices (four for each nation). When all nations have indicated, simultaneously, their choices of action, the outcomes can be announced immediately. The students are sure to gain further insight into the wisdom of their move by referring to a booklet that points out some of the consequences of each nation's decision.

A set of six simulation games called "American History Games" can be useful for eighth through twelfth grade students. They are called "Colony," "Frontier," "Reconstruction," "Promotion," "Intervention," and "Development." They cover American history from the relations between the American Colonies and Britain through the relationships of major world powers and developing countries. These games involve decision-making based on economics.[4]

"The Game of Empire," developed by the Education Development Center, is suitable for junior high school students. It

---

[3] *Simulation Games for the Social Studies Classroom*, pp. 22-23.
[4] Science Research Associates, 259 E. Erie St., Chicago, Illinois 60611.

is modeled on mercantilism and economic factors leading up to the American Revolution.[5]

"Market," a game for sixth-graders, has students play the roles of consumers and sellers. The game teaches the concepts of supply, demand, and price. It helps pupils learn not only economics, but also team cooperation.[6]

"Napoli," is a simulation game for junior high school students and older players. It illustrates the legislative process and the representative nature of democracy, but does not try to simulate the exact procedure of either house.[7]

"Superhighway"[8]

"Superhighway" is one very simple example of a good simulation game. It can be used with a transportation unit for fifth- or sixth-graders. It involves a crisis in a small town created by the construction of a new superhighway that will cut off the town and cause a serious decrease in business. The materials consist of a map of the area, character cards, decision cards, and final-result cards. The game begins with a study of the map of the area. Each child receives a character card, reads it silently, and tries to put himself in the position of the character. One child in each role reads the description of his character from his card to the class. Children with the same roles interact and discuss the problem. The mayor then calls a town meeting. Each player offers proposals and makes comments according to his own character's viewpoint. Then decision cards are distributed and pupils choose their decisions based on their characters and on the town meeting. Final-result cards are distributed corresponding to the decisions made.

Example of one decision card:

D. You believe in peaceful means of protest and therefore agree to join the picket line.

---

[5] KDI Instructional Systems, Inc., 1810 Mackenzie Dr., Columbus, Ohio.

[6] Abt Associates, Inc., 55 Wheeler St., Cambridge, Massachusetts 02138.

[7] Western Behavioral Sciences Institute, 1121 Torrey Pines Blvd., La Jolla, California.

[8] Barbara Bennon and Annette Cianfrini, "Superhighway — A Simulation Game," *Instructor* No. 6, LXXX, February, 1971, pp. 94-95.

Example of a corresponding final-result card with the consequences of the decision:

> D. Your method was justified and was a move in the right direction but was not successful. Your failure resulted from the fact that you represented one small town in opposition to larger forces.

"Skyjack" — A Sample Map and Globe Game

This sample game can be used for any bright fourth through sixth grade pupil. It will be suitable at all times during the school year for stimulating interest in maps or globes. Have children make the cards for the game, using the lists on pp. 187-190.

The game consists of the following materials:

1 large flat world map (or metal globe) marked with flight plans
2 packs of 54 cards
6 - 1/2" cardboard planes (with magnet bases for globe)
2 - 3/4" cardboard planes (with magnet bases for globe)
1 - cardboard spinner with 8 sections.

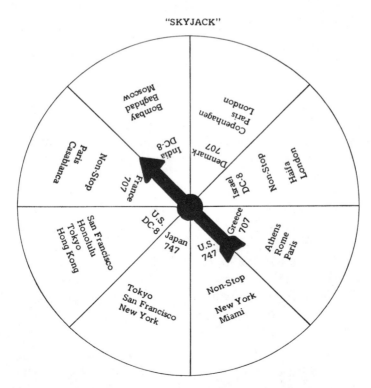

Figure 9-1

"Skyjack" can be played by two to eight players, with one of the packs of cards. The other pack is for variety when the game is played again.

One player begins the game by spinning the spinner which designates his flight plan and type of airplane. Each player spins in turn, taking the remaining flight plans and planes. If the pointer on the spinner lands on a line between two flight plan sections, the player spins again.

Players are seated around the map or globe. The first player begins the play by taking a card from the top of the pack. He must follow the directions on the card by finding the place and moving his plane to it, whether it fits his flight plan or not. The other players to his left follow in the same way. All cards are discarded after drawing, with these exceptions:

1. Armed guard cards (keep them to foil hijacks).

2. Anti-cholera serum cards (keep them in case of epidemic).

3. Cards to keep opponents from landing in Rome for two turns.

Players become familiar with cities other than **those** on their own flight plans, as they will have to make choices when they draw certain cards. For example, one card says:

Choose one of these for your next stop:

New York
Los Angeles
Paris
Bombay

When making a choice, if none of the cities listed are on a player's flight plan, he must choose the one closest to his next stop.

The game ends when one player makes his complete designated *round trip* flight on the map first. Extra stops or delays do not disqualify a player, as long as he makes all required stops.

If the pack of cards is used up without a winner, the player who has completed the most of his flight plan wins. In case of a tie, the winner is the player closest to his destination.

This game can be adapted for younger pupils by simplifying the flight plans to two stops. Substitute simpler words for the following: *destination, departure point, visibility, V.I.P., authori-*

ties, opponent, berserk, detention, cholera, quarantine, serum, overpowered, Air Controller, and *suspicious.*

The game can be used by older students if you extend the scope of the flight plans to include more exotic places. Lengthen the flight plans by adding to the number of stops.

"Skyjack" Card List — Pack 1

Land at San Francisco.

Go directly to your next destination. (9 cards)

Land at Rome. A hijacker has taken over your aircraft. Miss one turn.

Mechanical trouble. Return to your last stop for a new part.

Go to your next stop. (2 cards)

You cannot land because of a crash on the runway. Land at nearest airport.

You must return to departure point because of bad weather at all other fields.

Your plane has been hijacked. Land at Athens. Miss one turn. (2 cards)

ARMED GUARD CARD (PICTURE OF ARMED GUARD). THIS CARD CAN BE USED TO PREVENT ONE HIJACK. (2 cards)

Go to New York.

Go directly to Tokyo.

A hijacker has been overpowered on your way to Havana. Land at Miami. Miss one turn.

You cannot land at your destination. Air traffic conditions are bad. Go to your last stop.

You are stopped on runway because of fog. Miss one turn.

Land at Moscow.

Stop at Haifa for fuel.

Fly to your next two stops. (2 cards)

Your plane has been hijacked. Land at Havana. Miss one turn.

Land at Honolulu.

Fly directly to Casablanca.

Land at London.

Your plane is carrying anti-cholera serum. KEEP THIS CARD IN CASE OF CHOLERA EPIDEMIC. GOOD FOR *ONE* USE ONLY.

Land at Oslo.

Your plane has been hijacked. Land at Paris. Miss one turn.

Land at Copenhagen.

The Air Controller in Rome is your cousin. No opponent may land in Rome for *two* turns without your permission. KEEP THIS CARD FOR TWO TURNS.

YOU WIN. Go directly to all your stops until you reach your final destination. Return to your departure point, making all stops.

Your passengers have been quarantined due to a case of cholera. You are OUT OF THE GAME, unless you have a serum card.

Choose one of the following for your next stop: Havana, Amman, Miami, Copenhagen.

Land at Casablanca. A hijacker has taken over your aircraft. Miss one turn.

Stop at Bombay for fuel.

Go to Miami. All other airports are closed.

Your plane has been hijacked. Land at Amman. Miss one turn.

Poor visibility at destination. Return to last stop.

Stop at Stockholm for fuel.

A suspicious object has been found in your luggage. Delay departure for one turn.

Plane is not permitted to take off because of icing of wings. Wait one turn.

Choose one of the following for your next stop: Baghdad, Tokyo, New York, Paris.

Your plane has been hijacked. Land at Hong Kong. Miss one turn.

Your destination field has been closed because of war. Go back one stop.

Authorities are searching for a bomb because of a phoned threat. Miss one turn.

Choose one of the following for your next stop: Bombay, Copenhagen, Oslo, Miami.

"Skyjack" Card List — Pack 2

Stop at Stockholm for fuel.

Go directly to your next destination. (9 cards)

Your plane has been hijacked. Land at Baghdad. Miss one turn.

Stop at Haifa for fuel.

Fly to your next two stops. (2 cards)

ARMED GUARD CARD (PICTURE OF ARMED GUARD). THIS CARD CAN BE USED TO PREVENT ONE HIJACK. (2 cards).

Your plane has been hijacked. Land at Havana. Miss one turn.

Choose one of these for your next stop: Hong Kong, Athens, Bombay, Casablanca, Haifa.

Land at Oslo.

You know the president's brother. Move one of your opponent's aircraft to the city of your choice.

Land in Havana.

Forced landing because of mechanical trouble. Miss one turn.

Land at San Francisco.

Your plane has been hijacked. Land at Hong Kong. Miss one turn.

Go to your next stop.

YOU WIN. Go directly to all your stops until you reach your final destination. Return to your departure point, making all stops.

Land at Copenhagen.

Land at Honolulu.

You cannot land because of poor visibility. Return to your last stop.

Your plane has been hijacked. Land at Paris. Miss one turn.

You are carrying a V.I.P. *in a hurry.* You arrive at destination ahead of schedule. Take an extra turn.

Choose one of these for your next stop: New York, Los Angeles, Paris, Bombay.

Stop at Hong Kong.

Delay take-off because of storms. Miss one turn.

Your plane has been hijacked. Land at Athens. Miss one turn.

Go to New York.

Your passengers have been quarantined due to a case of cholera. You are OUT OF THE GAME, unless you have a serum card.

Fly directly to Casablanca.

Your plane is carrying anti-cholera serum. KEEP THIS CARD IN CASE OF CHOLERA EPIDEMIC. GOOD FOR *ONE* USE ONLY.

Go directly to Tokyo.

Authorities are searching for a bomb because of a phoned threat. Miss one turn.

Choose one of these for your next stop: San Francisco, Miami, Paris, London.

A baby has been born en route. Return to your last stop.

Your plane has been hijacked. Land at Amman. Miss one turn.

Your plane's baggage has been lost. Wait one turn.

Go to Miami. All other airports are closed.

Mechanical trouble. Return to your last stop for a new part.

A passenger has gone berserk and knifed someone. Return to your last stop for detention.

Your plane must delay take-off due to storms. Miss one turn.

Land at Budapest. A hijacker has taken over your aircraft. Miss one turn.

Choose one of these for your next stop: Rome, Los Angeles, Hong Kong, Tokyo.

Your plane has strong tail winds. Take an extra turn.

Choose one of these for your next stop: Oslo, Havana, Paris, New York.

Choose one of these for your next stop: Copenhagen, Haifa, Amman, Athens.

"Pollution — Life and Breath" —
A Sample Ecology and Health Game

This sample game can be used for any bright fourth through sixth grade pupil. It relates to health or ecology units. Children will enjoy making cards and discs for this game. They can use the lists on pp. 192-194.

The game consists of the following materials:

1 pack of 18 cards with red backs
1 pack of 18 cards with black backs
1 cardboard spinner with 8 sections
10 - life-point discs (value of 25 life points)
10 - life-point discs (value of 10 life points)
10 - life-point discs (value of 5 life points)

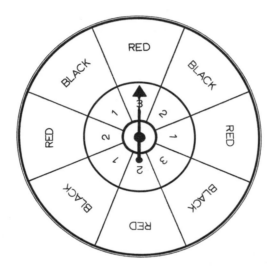

Figure 9-2

This game can be played by two to four players. One player acts as the dealer and banker. The dealer gives 100 life points in various values of discs and two red and two black cards to each player. Players read each card and choose the best black card and the best red card, discarding one black card and one red one. The play begins with the first player to the left of the dealer, who follows the directions on his remaining red and black cards, paying life points and receiving life points from the banker. He discards each card as he follows its directions. The other players do the same in turn. When it is the first player's turn again, he spins the spinner to see whether he takes a card from the red pack or from the black pack. The spinner also tells him how many cards he is to take, — one, two, or three. If the player draws more than one card, he must choose the one that is least valuable to him, to discard without using it. He follows the directions on the other cards that he keeps, and then he discards them.

The game ends when all of the cards are gone, or when one player has life points and all of the other players have lost theirs. The winner is the player with the most life points at the end of the game.

If the spinner tells a player to take black cards or red cards and that color of card is gone, the player waits until the next turn to play again. If the pointer on the spinner lands between colors, the player spins again.

You can adapt this game for younger pupils by simplifying the vocabulary. Eliminate words like *amplifier, pneumonia, refinery, temperature inversion, uninhabited,* and *chlorinated.* Replace them with simpler terms. For younger children, spend some time discussing the different kinds of pollution and the various things that damage our environment.

If you wish to adapt this game for older pupils, you will need to add at least ten more cards to each pack. Some of your gifted pupils will enjoy writing up the extra cards for the game as a special project. Have them read the 36 cards in the game. Make sure that they are aware of the difference between the red and black packs. Involve them in a lot of research to be sure to get plenty of variety in the 20 cards that they compose. They'll learn more from designing a game than they will from playing it.

"Pollution — Life and Breath" Card List — Red Pack

Swim in chlorinated pools. Avoid polluted lake. Win **ten** points.

Give up smoking at age 21. Win back 50 points.

Join a group that works to move city dump to **uninhabited** area. Win ten points.

Move from Los Angeles to a small farm town **in Iowa. Win 50** points.

Stop burning leaves. Win five points.

Clean rubbish from a nearby stream. Win 15 **points.**

Use lead-free gas in your car. Win five points.

Quit job in coal mine. Win back 40 points.

Move away from oil refinery. Win back 30 points.

Refuse to start smoking. Win 75 points.

Sell your electric guitar and amplifier. Win 30 points.

Move to an uninhabited area. Win 40 points.

Thunderstorm clears the air. Win five points.

Live at least 20 miles away from the city — away from factories and mines. Win ten points.

Take air-conditioned train instead of driving in heavy traffic every day. Win 30 points.

Move from Los Angeles to Chicago. Win five points.

Go for a long trip to an uninhabited mountain area. Win back five points.

Join a community group fighting pollution. Work actively to do everything you can. Win ten points.

"Pollution — Life and Breath" Card List — Black Pack

Swim in polluted lake ten times. Lose ten points.

Use gas with lead in your car. Lose 15 points.

Drive in heavy traffic daily. Lose 30 points.

Ride the subway daily. Lose ten points because of the noise.

You play an electric guitar with an amplifier. Lose 20 points because of the noise.

You have pneumonia. Lose 15 points.

You live near an oil refinery. Lose 40 points.

You live in the daily pollution of New York City. Lose 30 points.

You live in the daily pollution of Chicago. Lose 30 points.

Pollution warning signal today. Lose ten points.

Begin smoking one pack of cigarettes a day at age 50. Lose 25 points.

Red pollution alert. Lose 25 points.

Temperature inversion keeps pollution from blowing away. Lose 25 points.

You have asthma and you live in a city. Lose 25 points.

You live near an open city dump. Lose 20 points.

You work in a coal mine. Lose 40 points.

Begin smoking one pack of cigarettes a day at age 17. Lose 75 points.

You live in the daily pollution of Los Angeles. Lose 50 points.

How to Create Your Own Games to Meet Your Needs

There are many kinds of games that will be useful to you. You can design your own games that will stimulate gifted pupils to learn more about the units you are studying. Have these bright children help in any way they can.

If you choose a board game, there are unlimited possibilities in the shapes of the game. The drawings below illustrate only a few of these.

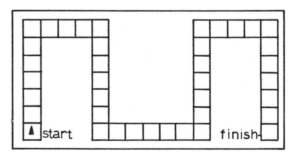

Figure 9-3

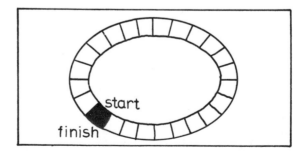

Figure 9-4

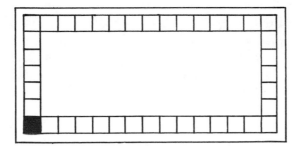

Figure 9-5

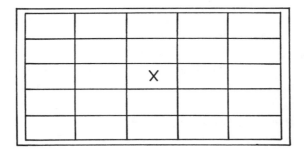

Figure 9-6

Figure 9-3 shows a typical board game in which the player begins with a token at the START space at the left and progresses by single or multiple jumps toward the FINISH space, the winner being the first to move his token to FINISH. Any device with numerals or dots will serve to give the players their number of moves. You may use a spinner, dice, or any thrower with numerals. You can use this type of game for almost any subject. For example, you may have questions or words to match on each board space. When a player lands his token on a certain space, he may not keep it there unless he answers the question or matches the word correctly. One player can serve as a checker with an answer card.

Figure 9-4 can be used in the same way as Figure 9-3.

Figure 9-5 uses the board format, but players are not trying to reach a FINISH space. They keep going around the board in much the same way as in "Monopoly."[9] They will receive points, discs, or play money as a reward for answering their questions. They may receive something for passing a certain point each time they go around the board. The winner will be the player who receives a set amount of points or play money first.

Another type of board is shown in Figure 9-6, which is the Lotto or Bingo type of board. With this form you generally have a caller, who calls out words or numbers so that players can cover squares, matching words, sounds, or any other answers to questions. Usually, players try to fill a row horizontally, vertically, or diagonally. The caller checks the row when a player has won.

Many games are played without a board. Players use cards or dominoes, matching pairs or trying to make runs of certain categories.

You can write your own simulation game for a social studies unit. For the first one, at least, try a game as simple as "Superhighway." (See page 184.) Choose a thought-provoking problem that will affect your characters in different ways. Write character cards that will show these varying points of view. When you write the character cards, give as much information as you can to make the characters real. You don't need names, but you must have ages, sex, and occupations. Describe how the game's problem affects the characters' lives, and give their personal viewpoints about it.

Your decision cards should cover every possible solution to the problem that any of your characters may decide on. Write a logical final-result card to match each decision.

The main element of success in this type of game is full understanding of the problem by the pupils, along with empathy for other characters' points of view. To accomplish this, you need to allow ample time for discussion among characters with the same roles, and at the town meeting where alternative solutions are discussed. The follow-up discussion after the simulation will be the most important one of all.

---

[9] "Monopoly," Parker Brothers, Inc., Salem, Massachusetts.

Simulation games can be time-consuming, but well worth it. They would make an excellent introduction to any unit, to stimulate interest. As culminating activities, they would help the students use and organize what they have learned, and interest them in studying further.

After you have written your game in rough form, test it by playing it. If it ends too quickly by someone winning too soon, you may need to adjust your rules. You may have too many wild cards, or players may have too few cards to dispose of. In a board game, your spinner or tosser may have numbers that are too high, giving players too many jumps each turn. You can make a game last a shorter time by adding wild cards, giving players less cards to play with, and raising the numbers on your spinner. You can adjust the length of time the game plays by writing special-direction cards that will delay players or move them faster toward their goal.

Almost any question-and-answer format can be applied to a game. To make it challenging for a gifted child, you will need some variety that you can add with wild cards or special-direction cards. See the section "What Makes a Game Fun?" on pages 180-181 for some of the many ways to add interest and challenge to games. While elements of chance are needed to make a game exciting, the game that will be the most valuable to a bright child is one that gives him an opportunity to plan and make choices. The more open-ended the game, the more actively he participates, the more a bright child will get from it.

CHECKLIST

Plan special games for bright pupils.

Use games that stimulate curiosity about ideas, objects, or places.

Provide games that require planning, choices, problem-solving, or role-playing.

Prevent boredom in the very bright by using games as clues to new interests.

Permit very bright pupils to do independent study instead of regular class lessons, unless you are teaching difficult new material.

Use chance, variety, and surprise, as these are some elements in making a game fun.

Use jokers or special-direction cards to add excitement to games.

Remember that gifted children enjoy games that require thought.

Schedule simulation games, which are excellent for bright pupils, because they provide chances for thinking, decision-making, role-playing, and discussion.

Create your own games to meet your needs by adapting samples of other games.

Use students' help in designing and writing up the games.

Index

199